The Enamels of China and Japan

The Enamels of China and Japan

CHAMPLEVÉ AND CLOISONNÉ

By Maynard G. Cosgrove

Illustrated with photographs in color

DODD, MEAD & COMPANY · NEW YORK

To Leota, *My Wife*

ISBN: 0-396-06733-6
Library of Congress Catalog Card Number: 72-7199
Printed in the United States of America
By Vail-Ballou Press, Inc., Binghamton, N.Y.

PREFACE

※ఆఆఆఆఆఆఆఆఆ※

$O_{N\ SUCH}$ a subject as the art of China and Japan, the prospective reader is entitled to a hint regarding the book's contents and its author's intentions. Some books do not need a preface— or would be better off without one—but that is not the case here. The present book may be described as an outline or digest, from an American point of view, of representative literature on the subject of Chinese and Japanese enamels. Because of the vast area involved under the head of general Oriental art, special care has been taken not to wander too far from the limits implied by this title, even to discuss the relative merits of similar work done in other countries.

A special reason for the book is that there seems to have been very little literature, written in English, on this subject within the past fifty years. Of the various books and articles written during the period of greatest popularity of Chinese and Japanese enamels— 1870 to 1915—they have long been out of print and are rarely available, even in the large-city libraries.

An appropriate subtitle for the book could be "The Tale of the Friendly Dragon." In the design of Chinese and Japanese enamels, the artist has combined the dragon along with the many different symbols of Longevity, Springtime, Happiness, etc. Each design tells a story. The owner of a piece of enameled ware cannot appreciate it unless he knows something of the process by which it was made and the meaning of the decoration—the iconography. According to tradition, the gift of a Chinese or Japanese object of art carries with it a wish for the good fortune implied by the symbols shown.

There is still much we do not know about this subject. A nugget of knowledge here, a fragment of often-debatable fact there—these items have been assembled and, it is hoped, arranged into a readable account. The purpose is to answer the questions so often asked about the kinds of enamels ordinarily encountered. It is more than likely there are mistakes, debatable and otherwise, scattered here and there, like the "clouds" in the background of a cloisonné vase.

There are many examples of Chinese and Japanese enameled ware in the United States, in museums and private collections. In quality and intrinsic value, they vary from excellent to "foreign trade stuff." There is also a great deal of ignorance on the subject, made up of about equal parts of misunderstanding and lack of appreciation.

In gleaning pertinent material for this book, it was necessary to examine a hundred or so volumes on the subject of Chinese and Japanese art. But there are large gaps in the available literature, confounded by often conflicting conclusions, apparently drawn in the attempt to fill these unexplained open spaces in the records. I found that no one library has more than half of the references cited in the bibliography; through the courtesy of interchange a library can usually borrow the others as reference books.

The superior numbers used throughout this book refer to the bibliography which is intended to present something more than a list of references. It commends those books and articles which are outstanding in the field of Oriental enamels, with my most profound appreciation of the sound research and study they represent. Each reference describes the nature of the contents enough to serve as a guide for those who may wish to seek a more detailed knowledge of the subject. The bibliography omits reference to many other books which masquerade under the catchy title of "Art," but which were apparently written not to educate but to criticize. The history of art in China and Japan offers a pitiless labyrinth to the misguided scholar, both writer and reader.

No attempt has been made to include photographs of Chinese and Japanese enameled ware which may be owned by American museums, because in those which were visited, few—sometimes no—pieces were on display. The one notable exception is the Springfield, Massachusetts Art Museum.[24] At the time of my study of the large collection (expertly displayed) in 1963, the individual pieces were not identified with respect to their Chinese or Japanese origin.

Maynard G. Cosgrove

CONTENTS

Preface   v
I. Political and Cultural Background   1
II. Glass and Enamels: Description   13
III. Glass and Enamels: History   19
IV. Chinese Enamels: Methods of Creation   28
V. Chinese Enamels: Design and Symbolism   37
VI. Chinese Enamels: The Conquest of Color   49
VII. Chinese Enamels in Relation to Other Arts
     of China   53
VIII. Japanese Enamels: Methods of Creation   63
IX. Japanese Enamels: Design and Symbolism   72
X. Color in Japanese Enamels   79
XI. Distinctions Between Chinese and Japanese
    Enamels   82
XII. Care and Cleaning of Enamels   86
     Appendices   89
        Chinese Dynasties and Dates   91
        Glossary   93
        Chinese Pronunciation   96
        Chinese-English List of Symbols   98
        Japanese-English List of Symbols   103
        Melting Points of Metals and Other Materials   107
     Bibliography   109
     Index   113

ILLUSTRATIONS

⁕⸰⸰⸰⸰⸰⸰⸰⸰⸰⸰⸰⸰⸰⸰⸰⸰⸰⸰⸰⸰⸰⸰⁕

Six plates showing steps in making
   cloisonné ware   *following page 4*
Details (enlarged) from teapot, showing enamel
   filling spaces between cloisons   *following page 4*
Incense burner, Chinese; champlevé on bronze   *facing page 21*
Rectangular box, Chinese   *facing page 21*
Vase, Japanese; rare example of work signed by
   Namikama   *facing page 52*
Pear-shaped copper teapot, Japanese   *facing page 53*
Plate, Japanese; copper cloisons on copper   *facing page 53*
Copper cup and saucer, Japanese   *following page 68*
Copper teapot, Japanese   *following page 68*
Vase, Japanese; silver cloisons on copper   *following page 68*
Bronze vase, Chinese   *facing page 84*

CHAPTER I

※٤٤٤٤٤٤٤٤٤٤

Political and Cultural Background

*I*N ORDER to understand and appreciate the history of art in China, it is necessary to know something of the political history of that vast and varying region.

In China's calendar, the venerable year 4668 corresponds to our relatively youthful 1970, which puts the beginning of her recorded history about 3000 B.C. At least the records tell of the original "Chinese" being in the Yellow River valley by that time, especially along the central and lower regions of the river, north to Manchuria, and west to the province of Kansu. Although in comparison with the beginning of what has been called "civilization" along the Nile River or the eastern shore of the Mediterranean, the development of the Chinese appears to have been a thousand years or more behind, its civilization has nevertheless remained essentially intact and relatively unchanged for more than four thousand years.

About 1700 B.C., the mysterious tribe of Shang, which may have come from northern or northeastern China, took over the region southeast of the present Peking. The Shang were in turn overthrown, about 1100 B.C., by the tribe of Chou, which spread farther south to the Yangtze River valley and west to the area now known as Yunnan province. The Chou dynasty, with a succession of 35 rulers, controlled the country until 255 B.C., when it was followed by the Ch'in and the Cheng dynasties. After a period of internal civil strife a new dynasty, Han, took over with Liu Pang becoming its first ruler or emperor in 206 B.C. The dynasty endured from 206 B.C. to A.D. 220, during which time China was enlarged on the south even to the jungles of Indo-China, north to the deserts of Mongolia, and west to the mountains of Tibet.

Also during the Chou, Ch'in, and Han dynasties there was a great advance in the level of culture, art, and living in general. It was during this period that the Huns, living far to the west of China, were warred upon and defeated; thus were opened up for the first time trade routes to the peoples of India, Arabia, and the Mediterranean countries. Through the centuries described, the area of China was extended from a single province to many, and the people making up these provinces were sometimes united, sometimes at war with each other.

Toward the end of the Han dynasty, there was increasing dissension. Later, there was a general disruption of the empire by the Huns from the west and various Tatar or Tartar tribes from the north. This general situation lasted during the period known as "The Six Dynasties," 220 to 589 A.D.

During most of the next two dynasties, Sui—589 to 618—and T'ang—618 to 907—the empire was reunited and continued the art and culture of the Han period. As early as A.D. 600, Chinese junks had ventured west to the Persian Gulf. Later, the Chinese traveled as far as the Red Sea, using camels as "freight trains" to carry goods to India, Arabia, and the West. Thus, we see that the Chinese knew something of the countries to the west and that these countries had learned something of China long before the celebrated travels of Marco Polo.

In spite of war from without and increasing dissension within the empire, especially during the latter half of the T'ang dynasty, Chinese art reached new heights, especially in painting, sculpture, and porcelain making which were sustained on into the thirteenth century.

Early in the thirteenth century, Mongolian tribes from northern Asia—in the vicinity of the Gobi—under the leadership of an obscure native named Temuchin—began an attack against northern China. By 1214, Temuchin had taken possession of most of the country north of the Yellow River and had given himself the title of Genghis Khan (also spelled Jenghis or Chinghis); Khan means literally lord or prince. The first Khan died in 1227, but in the meantime, his armies had been victorious in a series of battles and in wars reaching from the China Sea westward to the Dnieper River, north of the Black Sea. A good part of northern China had been taken by Genghis and given the name of Cathay, a name derived from the Tatar language.

Wars of various kinds dragged on for some sixty-five years. It was not until 1280 that the grandson of Genghis, Kublai Khan, gained control of the entire Chinese empire. Yet, in 1259, Kublai had founded the Yüan dynasty which held the Dragon Throne, as it was called, until 1368. By then, his race had become more Chinese than Mongolian. The Mongols have often been described as the "barbarians of the north"; their assimilation of Chinese culture and customs was exceedingly slow. While their sweeping conquest of China from their old capital of Karakorum, situated a thousand miles to the northwest of Peking, did not completely destroy the flourishing type of Chinese civilization they found, their occupancy wrought extensive changes in the arts and customs of the conquered country.

However, by the time of Kublai's death in 1294, there were many marvels created in China, far beyond anything Europe could claim. The world's first astronomical observatory, with its beautifully designed bronze instruments, was completed in Peking by 1279. The Great Wall of China had been completed before the arrival of Marco Polo. The last six hundred miles of the Grand Canal, between Peking and Nanking, were completed by Kublai. Water clocks had been installed on various bridges; movable type, for the printing of books, had been in use for centuries; paper money, in circulation in many sections of the empire, was one of the many wonders described by Polo. And, not least of the wonders, the beginning of glass enameling in this part of the world has been ascribed to the period of the Yüan dynasty.

A reading of *The Travels of Marco Polo* gives a first-hand insight into the China of the time. Polo arrived in Peking about 1275; he remained about sixteen years and departed in 1292, two years before Kublai's death.

After the death of Kublai Khan, the Mongolian (Yüan) dynasty deteriorated and was finally overthrown by a Chinese nationalist movement. The new and purely Chinese dynasty, the Ming, finally took over in 1368. Ming means *light*, especially as it pertains to the perfected spirit in mankind. This dynasty, which endured from 1368 to 1643, was the last to be controlled by pure Chinese. Under the seventeen emperors included in the dynasty, travel, traffic with other countries, culture, and the arts were encouraged—the result was a great advance in the quality and quantity of ceramics, lacquers, and the enamels which have been ascribed to this period.

Although many of the basic arts of China, such as bronzes, silks, and jade, were a thousand years or more old by the time of the Ming dynasty, they reached new heights of excellence during this period, especially in painted porcelain and enamels, in architecture, and in culture in general. However, after a couple of centuries under the Ming dynasty, China became increasingly weaker, due to political and military reasons, so that, by 1643, the dynasty was overthrown by invaders from Manchuria in the northeast. The Manchus or Tungus were a non-Chinese people, closely related to the Mongols.

The resulting Ch'ing dynasty, with a series of ten Manchu emperors, ruled until 1912, at which time the emperor and the Manchus as a governing race were themselves overthrown and China became a republic. At the same time, the pigtail, which the Chinese had been compelled to wear as a token of their domination by the Manchus, was no longer required; it had been degrading to them, but funny to the foreigner.

A fact to be kept in mind is that throughout the centuries during which China was a conquered nation, although dominated by foreign barbarians, it eventually managed to absorb them into their own culture rather than be changed by them. In art, the

Six plates showing steps in making cloisonné ware. Left to right above: ink drawing on metal ground, cloisons secured in place, first filling with enamel and firing. Below: second filling and firing, third filling and firing, and (final step) grinding and polishing of enamel down to level of cloisons.

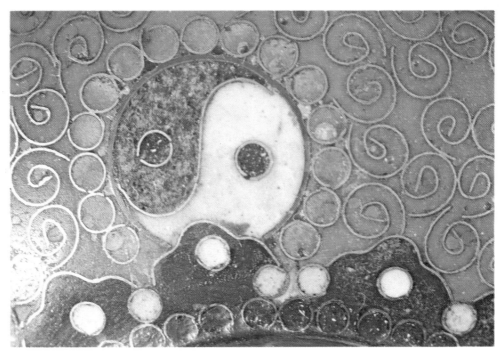

Details (enlarged) from teapot, showing enamel filling spaces between cloisons.

Chinese preserved their own ideals and conceptions. They owe little or nothing to any other country; to whatever influences they did accept, they invariably gave a Chinese accent. The question is often raised as to whether and to what extent the Chinese or Japanese artist borrowed from Persian, European, or even Mayan art. A little more attention to the historical background of China should indicate the relative unimportance of this question.

JAPAN

With regard specifically to Japan, it is necessary to give a brief review of the events prior to the first knowledge by the western countries of the work done by Japanese artists.

From the beginning of the nineteenth century, various foreign countries, including Russia, Holland, and the United States, had tried to open trade relations with Japan. Entirely due to their own fault, they did not succeed except to a very limited extent. The feudal system which had existed in Japan for eight hundred years finally came to an end in 1871, a condition which had been antagonistic to the development of trade or friendly relations with other countries. In contrast to the history of art in China, that of early Japan has been difficult to learn.

In 1853 and 1854, Commodore Perry—acting under orders from Washington—obtained a treaty of peace and friendship, which was to become the opening wedge to more diplomatic and commercial concord, not only with the United States but with other countries.

It was not until 1867, when Japan brought a magnificent collection of its art work to the Paris Exhibition, that western Europe had a chance to see and to appreciate the excellence displayed in every branch of its artistic techniques. Following the Paris Exhibition, there was an increasing demand—a craze for anything Japanese, including enamels—which did not taper off until well into the twentieth century.

During this period, the United States showed its appreciation and desire for Japanese enameled ware, such as those pieces in the

George Walter Vincent Smith Collection in the Springfield (Mass.) Art Museum and other museums. As a substitute for an examination of this collection, the two volumes by James L. Bowes provide an excellent source of study in text and illustration.

A large part of the material included in the following chapters regarding Chinese enamels applies equally well to the design and methods of making enameled ware in Japan. There are differences in conception, design, workmanship, and use, which are of interest to the collector. A knowledge of these differences is essential to an understanding and appreciation of the art of both countries. Chinese wares are generally held in higher esteem than Japanese wares; there may be a reasonable basis for this evaluation but it will not be discussed here.

The records indicate that the earliest enamels were made in Japan about 1604, at the beginning of the Tokugawa Shogunate. At this time, the shogun (a military governor) was the virtual ruler of the country and this continued to be so until the revolution of 1867, when the emperor regained the control due his rank. For a long time prior to 1603, Japan had been in a state of war and thus much more interested in the metal work relating to swords and bows and arrows. Sword hilts and sword guards were decorated in incised designs, in gold and silver or various alloys; a branch of Japanese art which continued down through the centuries.

As a result of their exceptional ability in the decoration of metal on metal, the Japanese artisan had the necessary experience to take up the exacting craftsmanship of making cloisonné enamels. The inherent trait of the Japanese to attempt designs and methods involving the greatest difficulty has not always been appreciated outside of Japan. Whereas, in the West, a piece of art may be appraised according to its artistic effect, in the East, especially Japan, it is valued in accordance with its merits as an example of superb craftsmanship.

Although the art of enameling on metal was supposed to have traveled from China to Japan by way of Korea, there is little in the way of tangible proof. The arts of Korea—in bronzes, pottery, porcelains, and painting—are similar to and undoubtedly derived from Chinese work. While it is true that Korean art is also similar to that of Japan, in design, form, and workmanship, it is far from clear which way this art traveled.

Korean animal figures are similar to those found in Chinese work. Similar flowers—such as peony, chrysanthemum, magnolia, and others—were made a part of their designs. Chinese civilization spread into neighboring Korea as early as 400 B.C., bringing with it a highly developed metal culture, especially in bronzes. Later, during the Han dynasty, a Chinese administration was established there. The records indicate that enameling was done in Korea as early as the sixteenth century.

Many of the various art treasures which were found in Japanese temples were importations from China. The temple Shoso-in, in the ancient city of Nara, contained some of the most famous. As is the case with so much of Chinese art, there is a general lack of identifying mark or any kind of record. The results of various intensive investigations of the art treasures in Japanese temples and monasteries are discussed in considerable detail by Sir Harry Garner and James L. Bowes—see the bibliography. There is apparently a wide disparity of opinion among European writers regarding the source and age of certain important pieces of enameled work.

The earliest Japanese enamels were apparently made in Kyoto, the greatest quantity in Nagoya. Later, Tokyo became a center of manufacture. The Harata family of Kyoto is usually credited with the first Japanese ornamentation of sword guards, early in the seventeenth century. Later members of the family are credited with the making of vessels with cloisonné designs. In addition to the above writers, the articles by Professor Jiro Harada are of special importance.

It now becomes necessary to explain, based on the most reliable information available, why practically all Japanese enameled wares are less than 140 years old—almost all of them less than one hundred years old. The available records indicate that, in the art of enameling on metal—as in cloisonné work—the technical knowledge and experience were lost in some way during the eighteenth century.

EXCERPTS FROM CHINESE AND JAPANESE AUTHORITIES

During the Ming dynasty, travelers from distant lands, mainly Europeans, arrived in large numbers in the various cities of China. The obvious superiority of such items as Chinese porcelains created a limitless demand in the export trade.

The various reports and opinions, which were turned out at great length by the returning travelers, can be found to be of general interest. Briefly, the consensus was to the effect that "the heathen Chinee was a quaint lot, even if they did turn out some fantastic wares." For this reason the writer believes it would not be amiss to summarize some of the offsetting statements made by those best in a position to know what they are talking about— the Chinese and the Japanese.

First of all, it is necessary to keep in mind that there is about the same difficulty getting information on the subject of Japanese enamel making as there is on Chinese work, and the same degree of conflict among the various writers, both native and foreign. With respect to both countries, therefore, more stress has generally been placed on design and methods of making the ware than on the frustrating puzzles relating to source and date.

It should be clear that no Occidental is qualified to pass judgment on the aesthetic or intrinsic value of any of the various arts of either China or Japan, unless he first rids himself of his preconceived notions of what constitutes "art." At the same time, he should study, with what is loosely called an "open mind," the background and the objectives of the Chinese and the Japanese artist. Much time and energy have been spent trying to interpret the laws of Chinese art; for example, see the following citations in the bibliography: Stephen W. Bushell, Arnold Silcock, and William Willette. These "laws" were found to be a combination of myth, legend, rules, inscriptions, and a precise system of symbolism. The resulting confusion and disagreement among certain scholars in the West provides more heat than light.

The following excerpt is part of a clipping taken from a Shanghai newspaper in 1923, which was found in a copy of the exceedingly rare volume by James L. Bowes.[4] In it, the owner of a valuable collection of Chinese bronzes, Mr. Chen Lin-son gave an interview to "The Idler," which seems pertinent to the present discussion.

> So frequently the people, especially those of the present day, do not either have time to view such collection, or if they have, they cannot appreciate the Chinese legends which are intimately associated with each piece. We Chinese have a curious feeling that we are continually being—shall I say criticized—by the western nations for our veneration of things ancient.

A similar statement is taken from an article by the Japanese art critic, Jiro Harada: [13]

> Occidentals have failed to a great extent to appreciate the true meaning of the Japanese creations. To really understand a civilization entirely different than one's own is an arduous and sometimes impossible job even to the Japanese themselves. The Japanese artist endeavors to present the poetic aspect in which the object appeals to his own refined and aesthetic imagination. But it is people's taste that often determines a vital point in art. The difference in the point of view from which East and West appraise and appreciate an art object is another factor which may have serious effects. In Japan the object is admired or condemned chiefly on its own intrinsic merits without regard to its decorative appeal.

Sheldon Cheney, in his treatise, *A World History of Art*, Viking, New York, 1946, states:

> Some commentators explain Oriental art as primarily symbolic. Even Japanese writers have emphasized this explanation as a bridge between Eastern achievement and Western enjoyment; and indeed Japanese painting and sculpture are far more marked with symbolism than the Chinese. Oriental art is not realistic or reproductive.

So far as can be learned, the best qualified authority on the subject of Japanese enamels is Jiro Harada.[13] In a series of articles appearing in *International Studio* he gave a realistic account of Metal Work, Wood and Ivory Carving, Painting, and Cloisonné Enamels. It is unfortunate that his writings on the above named subjects do not appear in book form or in any available encyclopedia. The following excerpt is taken from Vol. 44, which contains a beautifully illustrated series on enamels:

> Cloisonné enamels are known amongst the Japanese by the name of *shippo*, a contraction of two words: *shichi*, denoting seven, and *ho*, meaning treasures. Some authorities endeavor to trace the term to an old Buddhist book, discrediting the Chinese origin on the strength of this particular ware being referred to in some old Chinese books as "ware of devil's country," suggesting thereby they were of foreign importation. However, it is obvious that the name *shippō* has been thought most appropriate in Japan, inasmuch as the exquisite beauty of the work gave it the appearance of having been wrought with the seven precious things, commonly known to consist of gold, silver, emerald, coral, agate, crystal, and pearl. The term *shippō* is used by Sōami to record the fact that Ashikaga Voshimasa, in the second quarter of the fifteenth century, had considered it superior to inlaid work. Many claim that the ware had been christened *shippō yaki*, or Dutch ware, by Kaji Tsunekichi and others, when a piece of it, falling into his hand, led to his discovery of this art after years of hard labour, and to the manufacture in 1832 (or 1839 according to some accounts) of a plate six inches in diameter, the first piece of modern cloisonné enamel as we know it today.

The following excerpt is taken from Vol. VII of a treatise by Frank Brinkley, *Japan & China*, Millet of Boston, 1901 and 1904:

> But there are apparently no means of determining the exact date of when champlevé and cloisonné enamel had its origin in Japan. One thing, however, is certain, namely that until the nineteenth century enamels were employed by the Japanese decorators for accessory purposes only. No such things were manufactured as vases, plaques, censers, or bowls having their surfaces covered with enamels applied either in the champlevé or the cloisonné style. In other words, none of the objects to which European and American collectors give the name "enamels" was produced by a Japanese artist prior to the year 1838.

If, as discussed by Bowes [4,5] and Garner [10] cloisonné enamels were made in Japan prior to 1832 (or 1838), why is there little mention of the work done, except a few hazy references to the "ancient treasures" in the royal palaces and temples—specimens which were admittedly rare and not available to the public? It could be that the references are to articles, while made prior to 1832 and classified as cloisonné, were either imports from China or inlaid sword guards having a minute portion in cloisonné decoration.

In his book published in 1895, Mr. James L. Bowes [5] makes the following statement:

> The origin, the time and place of manufacture, the process employed in the fabrication of these marvels of workmanship, and the uses to which the vessels were put, appear to be now unknown in Japan, and the records of the country, so far as they have been available, are silent on these points.

The lack of records has been stressed because the question most frequently asked in reference to enameled ware—Chinese or Japanese—is: How old is it? Is it an antique? In the evaluation of this kind of art, other factors are much more important. It is a rare occasion when even a piece of Chinese enamel, made prior to 1830, is seen outside of a museum.

Prior to 1967, a law of the United States Congress stipulated that any import, in order to be considered an antique, must be proven to have been made before 1830 (supposedly, the beginning of the age of machinery). It should be noted that in England the definition of an antique is somewhat different and more flexible. The Antiques Appraiser, U.S. Customs Service, Port of New York, was asked what method his office used in order to learn the date of manufacture, with special regard to Chinese and Japanese works of art. Nothing tangible on the subject was obtained. Later in 1967, the U.S. Customs Service law was revised to define any object that is one hundred years old as an antique; as of 1970, this would mean any article manufactured prior to 1870.

According to Jiro Harada [13], the Paris Exposition of 1900 created an especially heavy demand for Japanese cloisonné enamels, which continued to the close of the St. Louis World's

Fair in 1904. With the increase in demand and production, there was a corresponding decrease in quality—which probably accounts for much of the inferior work still to be found on the market. It is reasonable to assume that the period of highest quality manufacture extended from 1840 to 1900. The claim by certain writers that the availability of high-quality ware, old or new, tapered off long before 1900, becomes a highly debatable matter of opinion and depends on the criteria used.

At the present time, the two principal companies still producing attractive cloisonné ware are The Inaba Cloisonne Company and the Ando Cloisonne Company, Ltd.; both have plants in Tokyo and Nagoya. The following excerpt is taken from a pamphlet (1965) entitled *History of Ando's Cloisonne:*

> "Shippo," the Japanese word for cloisonné, literally means "seven heavenly treasures" and presumably originated in a Buddhist sutra in the expression "Just like the treasure of seven jewels." The jewels vary according to the different sects, but generally the seven which include gold, silver, emerald, agate, coral, crystal, and pearl are regarded as standard. Modern Japanese industrial art craft developed remarkably from about the middle of the 19th Century.
>
> It was arousing that Tsunekichi Kaji (1803–1883), the second son of a Samurai living in the suburbs of Nagoya, succeeded in making a small container, 5″ high after experimenting for six years.
>
> Kaji's foremost contribution was his dividing of the vertical placing of delicate ribbon-like silver lines on the surface of the base metal, whereby the outline of patterns was firmly made.
>
> An illustration in the accompanying catalog shows a vase with a quite intricate design—described as "high class ancient pattern." It is similar to a "cabinet vase" of the Ming dynasty, described as "long necked, purple, cloud vase" but is entirely enameled in a single color; only the neck has a graceful design of "cloud" cloisons. The height of this vase is 10½ inches and the catalog price (in 1965) was 150,000 yen; at $2.78 per 1000 yen, the equivalent price was $417.00.

CHAPTER II

Glass and Enamels: Description

*A*S NEARLY as can be determined, all of the enamels used by the Chinese and Japanese, in the art of decorating metal and ceramic work, consist of a vitreous composition—meaning that they are derived from glass. Accordingly, a general knowledge of glass is necessary to a proper appreciation of enamels. Indeed, enamel *is* glass, colored or colorless—transparent, translucent, opaque, or opalescent. Whether translucent or opaque, enamel is essentially glass to which appropriate metal oxides have been added to reduce the melting point and to obtain the desired colors. It is then placed in paste form on the metal or ceramic base and fused there, forming a very thin and fragile decoration.

Nature made a form of glass, known as obsidian, some half billion years ago, by means of the rapid cooling of hot lava, containing silica, as spewed from volcanoes. But the most common materials on earth—probably 90 per cent or more of the total —can be used in making glass: silica, soda, lime or limestone, lead oxide, etc. Thus man-made glass is to be found in a great many varieties. Only basic glass will be discussed here.

GLASS

The composition of the glass, whether in a plain glass window, a "stained glass" window or in an enamel, is essentially the same, the color being obtained by the addition of a specific metal oxide to the colorless glass. The basic ingredient of all glass is silica—ordinary clean sand. Quartz (a principal part of granite) is silica in crystalline form and silica sand is quartz that has been ground into small, loose grains by the forces of nature working through millions of years. Although quartz has a high melting point (3110°F.), it has the peculiar property of fusing at much lower temperatures when mixed with various combinations of lime, soda, potash, and borax. In these mixtures, the silica component ranges from 50 to 75 per cent of the total. The kinds and relative proportions of the other ingredients determine the nature of the resulting glass.

The simplest "glass" is only fused quartz. The higher the quartz component, the higher the temperature required for melting or fusing. Ordinary modern glass contains silica—about 72 per cent; soda—13 to 18 per cent; lime—5 to 8 per cent; magnesium—0 to 4 per cent. The melting point of glass can vary from 1800° to 2900° Fahrenheit. The ingredients in lead crystal glass are silica—56 per cent; lead oxide—31 per cent; potash—12 per cent. Although an alkali, such as soda or potash, is an essential component of glass, it may be derived from various sources—niter or ashes of seaweed, for example—depending on what is available at a given location.

In the fifteenth century B.C., the glassmakers found that the presence of antimony as a component had an amazing effect on the process; it produced opaqueness in the glass. Then, about the sixth century B.C., it was discovered that if the temperature were raised during the melting, the antimony could convert an opaque white into a crystal-clear transparency. Beginning about the fourth century after Christ, manganese replaced antimony as a decolorant. Thus the presence of one or the other in an article of glass provides a clue to determination of its age.

Two ingredients used in glassmaking sound somewhat alike but serve distinctly different purposes. Magnesium oxide (or magnesia) may be used in different proportions according to the type and properties of the glass desired; about 2 per cent for plate glass,

4 per cent or more for ordinary window glass and 0 to 3.5 per cent for tableware. Manganese is used, as stated above, to change the color of the glass from opaque white to clear, or—in the form of manganese silicate—to provide a rich purple tone.

In recent years, much of the guesswork regarding place of origin and age has been taken out of the study of ancient glass and glass-enamel ware. The artisan had to proceed by trial and error, but there is no doubt that, thanks to his Oriental patience, he persevered in endless experimentation. By the use of new and highly sensitive chemical analysis—and the use of the spectroscope and X-ray fluorescence—a precise determination can usually be made of the various ingredients and proportions used in making an item of glass. A small sample, ground off an inconspicuous part of a glass vessel, is studied by spectroscope as it is being burned in a carbon-arc flame. By this means, for example, it has been found that Roman glass of the time of Christ consistently contained about one per cent magnesium oxide and less than one-half per cent potassium oxide. At about the same time, glass from the ancient valleys of Mesopotamia contained four or five times as much of each of these ingredients. Ray Winfield Smith[23] has written an explicit account of the methods used; it suggests that an analysis can be made whenever a wisp of glass powder can be removed from an inconspicuous place on the item being studied.

ENAMELS

As used in this study, the word "enamels" refers to the application of decorative designs in glass to a metal (sometimes ceramic) surface, which is then fused into place. The resulting product has been named "champlevé enamel" or "cloisonné enamel." Both terms—"champlevé" and "cloisonné"—are adjectives, describing their respective methods used, although, by common usage, they are often employed as nouns. Champlevé means that the surface of the metal is chiseled out or engraved, so that the enamel can be laid in the depressions. The term cloisonné means "inlaid between partitions or fences"—that is, designs outlined with bent wire fillets or strips. These methods will be discussed in detail in a later chapter.

Enamels will vary in melting temperature, brilliance, viscosity under heat, and in final hardness according to the kinds and proportions of the ingredients used in the glass, plus the oxides added to provide color. The metal oxide is added to the glass while it is in a molten state. Because of the countless combinations possible, the precise formula used to create a certain result is difficult to ascertain. It may be for this reason (and the risk involved) that so few writers on the subject have given this phase of the problem its proper due, see Ray Winfield Smith.[23] Even so, it must be difficult for a critic to appraise the aesthetic qualities of enamel work without a knowledge of how it was done. The following brief outline is based primarily on the detailed account to be found in the excellent book by Oppi Untracht.[25]

The basis for all enamels is the frit or flux, meaning the clear glass. Variations in the composition of the frit result in an enamel of varying viscosity under heat and hardness or brilliance on cooling. Borax and soda or potash control the elasticity of the enamel; a proper balance between these two elements is required to bring the coefficient of expansion and contraction of the enamel close to the metal—during and after the firing in the kiln. Otherwise, the enamel would not adhere to the metal and would crack or pop off the metal on cooling.

The process of making an enamel consists of two principal steps: (1) making the glass base or frit; (2) adding to the frit various metal oxides while the glass is in a state of fusion (melted) to obtain the required color. Both of these steps require painstaking care. The following description covers only the second step.

One method is to take the flux or colorless glass, heat pieces of it to a dull reddish glow and drop them into cold water, where they will shatter into small fragments. Then, by one means or another, the glass fragments are pounded and ground down into a fine powder. To obtain a particular color, a small amount of metal oxide—from 2 to 4 per cent—is added to a portion of the glass powder, the mixture melted, cooled to a solid by dropping it into water and the process of grinding repeated to obtain the enamel powder. A temperature of from 1800° to 2300° is required in the smelting furnace in order to melt the mixture. It will be noted below, however, that with the addition of the oxide, the final enamel as used will have a lower melting point.

The color and characteristics of the enamel may be changed by an endless combination of components, proportions, temperature used in fusing, and the care with which the melting conditions are maintained. This rule applies not only to the basic frit but to the enamel. A different shade of color cannot be produced simply by mixing two enamels. Most enamels look completely different in powder form and when fired. It may be assumed that the artisan makes up enough samples in color to eliminate any disappointing surprises in the final result.

A transparent enamel can be changed to opaque white by the addition of tin oxide. The addition of antimony or uranium produces yellow or orange; gold oxide produces red; manganese produces purple; copper oxide is used for green; platinum for gray; iridium for black.

Enamels may be classified into three principal groups; opaque, translucent, and transparent. A fourth group, giving an opalescent effect, is obtained by varying the degree of opacity and translucence. Opaques, translucents, and opalescents were and are most often used on a copper or bronze base. Transparents are best for silver or gold. Each of the various enamels to be used on a metal or ceramic base must have approximately the same melting point. In addition, when a metal base is used, the fusing points of the enamels must be lower than that of the base to which they are applied. The melting point of enamels ranges from 1450° to 1560°F. The melting point of silver, bronze, and copper ranges from 1640° to 1981°F.

Apparently very little was written to accompany the wondrous works created during the Ming and later dynasties. If such records had been available, the various writers on this category of

Chinese art would have undoubtedly covered the subject in much better detail. In his *Chinese Art*, "Preface to First Edition," Dr. Bushell[6] wrote:

> During a residence of some thirty years at Peking I have been a diligent collector of Chinese books relating to antiquities and art industries and tried to gain a desultory (sic) knowledge of their scope. There is such a vast amount of Chinese literature on every conceivable subject, of all shades of authenticity, that one of the chief difficulties of the student is that of selection.

Even a brief perusal of Dr. Bushell's books will indicate how far from "desultory" was his research and his grasp of Chinese art in all its branches.

CHAPTER III

Glass and Enamels: History

G*LASS* is one of the most ancient of man-made creations. There are various stories purporting to describe the discovery of making glass; certainly it was accidental. The earliest man-made glass was in the form of colored glazes, which the ancient Egyptians used to decorate stone and pottery. As nearly as can be determined, some of this work dates back to about 3000 B.C. or earlier.

The principal change in the making of glass and enamels during the past two thousand years and more is in the increased precision used in the measurement of the ingredients. A detailed description of the methods used in determining the various formulas is contained in a recent article by Ray Winfield Smith in the *National Geographic Magazine*.[23] However, since the chemistry of glassmaking in ancient times was based strictly upon trial and error—as to source of materials, proportions of the ingredients used, and the methods of making—the conclusions cannot be as precise as we should like.

As nearly as can be determined, the Egyptians were making various kinds of vessels of glass as early as 1500 B.C. This early glass was so scarce and so precious that it was reserved entirely for royalty. Glass was made in various countries around the eastern Mediterranean, especially in ancient Greece, Persia, and Rome, from the sixth century B.C. to the tenth century after Christ.

Glazes were also used in Greek sculpture to give special effects, from the first century to the fifth, and Greek goldsmiths inlaid flowers or other small designs of glass in their work, in blue or white enamel, similar to cloisonné work.

Glassmakers in antiquity were an itinerant group, moving from place to place according to varying circumstances. Analysis of glass samples indicates that there was widespread travel between the Mediterranean countries and ancient central and southern Asia. Glassmakers found that certain substances in nature, such as rock, sand, earth, or ashes, gave special effects or properties to the finished article. By comparing the chemical analysis of an unidentified glass sample with that of glass samples having a known history, the age and origin of the former can sometimes be ascertained quite definitely; otherwise, this part of the investigation remains difficult. For more details of the problem, see item 23 of the Bibliography.

Early records of the Celts, in the British Isles, indicate that they did enamel work in about the third century. Later, during the period from the sixth century to the ninth, the Celts and the Saxons produced numerous examples of poured molten glass, the colors mainly lapis blue, red, and white. It has been suggested, because of the close resemblance in method, style, and colors, that this type of glassmaking was transferred somehow from Ireland or England to Byzantium—later called Constantinople, and today Istanbul.

The ancient walled city of Byzantium became the center for a great deal of excellent enamel work, using gold and silver. The art was at its best from the ninth century to the eleventh century. The Byzantine enamels were of the cloisonné rather than the earlier champlevé type. Beaten gold was often used; in some work the cloisons (the metal strips or partitions) were not more than 1/100 inch thick. Existing examples indicate Persian derivation, or influence.

Enamel work, in cloisonné or champlevé—sometimes in combination—was being done in Germany from the tenth century to the fourteenth. It was not until about the thirteenth century that Ven-

Incense burner, Chinese, champlevé on bronze. Stylistic dragons with devildog finial.

Rectangular box, Chinese. Lotus blossom pattern over bare metal (bronze).

ice was to become the most renowned source of glassmaking as we know it, but it was always in the form of vessels rather than in enamel work. For those who are interested in the art of these countries—Egypt, the Byzantine Empire, Italy—an exceptionally fine collection of ancient glass wares may be seen in the Toledo Art Museum.

Just when the art of glassmaking and enameling reached China is not known and there is a decided difference of opinion among those who have attempted to learn the facts. Dr. Bushell [6] states that, according to precise data compiled by historians of Northern and Southern China (which were two separate kingdoms at the time), the Chinese probably knew about the making of glass and imported glass from about the fifth century. Others insist that glass was made in parts of China as early as the last two centuries B.C., being imported in the form of small ingots and reworked into beads and other small objects—sometimes modified with certain native minerals. The records of the Han dynasty refer to the importation of glass among other things brought from the West, probably from Alexandria and other Mediterranean sources. A Chinese historical work reports that opaque glass in ten different colors was being imported in the late Han dynasty.

There is no authentic record that glass enamel work (on metal) was done much before the thirteenth century. It appears plausible that China was not much interested in the use of glass in the making of vessels, when it had been producing wares of much more durable materials for a thousand years or more, such as bronze, lacquers, jade, and ivory. One theory has it that the introduction of glassmaking into China was related to or somehow the result of the Mongolian invasion westward to the shores of the Black Sea and almost to ancient Byzantium. In this way, examples of Byzantine and Persian art, especially in enamels, and probably the artisans themselves, were brought back to eastern China. Item 18 of the Bibliography provides in its series of maps a very clear picture of the vast extent of the Mongolian empire during the thirteenth and fourteenth centuries.

The Mongolian conquests helped to spread man's ideas and

knowledge in the arts and sciences because of the Mongols' curiosity and desire for this kind of culture. An excellent description of China and its peoples, both native and foreign, is presented in the narrative of Marco Polo, who spent so large a part of his life among the fantastic wonders of Cathay. Although the Mongols may have had a part in bringing China into a new type of art—the use of glass and enamels of glass—it is remarkable that the Chinese absorbed the invaders as a race and gave them a civilization they did not previously possess.

It is generally agreed that the earliest (and, some say the most famous) enamels, both champlevé and cloisonné, were made just prior to and during the Ming dynasty. Because the various forms of Chinese art are related to each other, at least in concept and design, it is interesting to keep in mind the chronological background of the principal divisions:

Cast bronze and silks	At least 2000 years B.C.
Carved jade	Centuries before the Christian era
Classical painting	Before A.D. 600
Porcelain, plain	First made during the T'ang dynasty
Porcelain, polychrome	First made during the Ming dynasty
Lacquer, as decoration	Early in the sixth century

Many features of design, symbols, and color were common to two or more of these diverse arts and were later brought into enameling.

The Chinese had been expert artists, unsurpassed in the design and making of bronze ware, for two thousand years before the advent of glass enameling. Despite the continually turbulent history of that part of the world, the Chinese used their inherent sense of art and craftsmanship in mastering this art of enameling, just as they had become masters in other media. Moreover, regardless of the medium, the Chinese always evolved a conception and symbolism of design uniquely their own. Of general books on this subject, the best by far is *Chinese Art* (two volumes) by Dr. S. W. Bushell.[6] Long out of print, any one of several editions will be found invaluable as a source of authentic facts. His work is unusually free of the boring essays of the not-too-inquiring critic.

The subject of Chinese enamel work becomes especially intriguing when the unsurpassed excellence of design and workmanship is contrasted with the unaccountable lack of authentic records regarding the history of the artists, descriptions of the methods used, and the symbolism involved. In addition, the great mass of expository efforts turned out by writers foreign to China can be boiled down to a small concentrate of factual and reliable data.

The original native Chinese term for enamels made with glass was "Fu-lin ware" or "Falan." The exact meaning of these terms has always been a subject of controversy—whether they referred to the source of the enamels, such as Byzantium, Arabia, or Persia, or whether they meant merely that the enamel was an import "from the devils' country," as the Chinese referred to foreign lands.

The attempt to learn just when enamel wares and processes first reached China is almost as futile as to guess why there should be a lapse of centuries between the purported introduction of glassmaking and the beginning of true enameling (on metal). For example, it is still debatable whether enamel work on metal was begun during the last few years of the Yüan (Mongol) dynasty or not until sometime after the inception of the Ming (Chinese) dynasty in 1368.

Moreover, it should be kept in mind that in the dating of a large part of the early cloisonné enamels, it has been difficult to determine whether they were actually made during the Ming dynasty, or a later one. The reasons for this frustrating situation will be discussed later.

A much-quoted source of information on the development of enameling in China is found in the 1459 edition of a well-known book on Chinese antiquities (first published in 1387), the *Ko ku yao lun,* translated as *Discussion of the Principal Criteria of Antiquities.* Therein is described "Kuei kuo yao," meaning "ware of the devils' country" or enamel ware which "resembles the cloisonné work of Fo-lang." The following excerpt appears under the heading of "Arabian ware":

> The actual place of production of what is known to us as Arabian kiln-burnt ware is not known. The body of the piece is made of copper, decorated with designs in colors made of various materials fused together. It resembles the cloisonné enamel work of Fo-lang. We have seen urns for burning incense, vases for flowers, round boxes with covers, wine cups, and the like, but they are fit only for use in the ladies' inner apartments, being too gaudy for the libraries of scholars of simple tastes. It is also called the ware of the devils' country (*Kuei kuo yao*). In the present day, a number of natives of the province of Yunnan have established factories in the Capital (Peking) where the wine-cups are made which are commonly known as "inlaid work of the devils' country." The similar enamels now at Yunnanfu, the provincial capital, are fine, lustrous, and beautifully finished.

This translation is taken from Dr. Bushell's books "Chinese Art" [6] and brings up several questions illustrating the difficulty of learning the pertinent facts of Chinese art. For example, the province of Yunnan, in southwest China, always was and still is the only province of that name in China. It is located at least fourteen hundred miles from Peking. The capital of the province was Yunnanfu (as mentioned in Dr. Bushell's translation); it is now known as Kunming. But the Rand McNally map [18] of the period around 1294 shows that when Marco Polo was sent by the "Great Khan" as "his embassador to the West," he was to go as far southwest as the province of Yunnan and its capital, Tali—a city west of Yunnanfu. In other words, these two references disagree as to which city was the capital. More important, the province of Yunnan lies far from the trade routes existing at the time of the excerpt taken from Dr. Bushell's book—which brings up the question: How did the "natives" learn enough about the manufacture of enamel ware to go to Peking and establish factories?

In any case, the resulting work was far superior in design and workmanship to anything produced prior to that time by any western country and this statement loses little of its significance because of the fact the Byzantine enamelers used mostly gold, while the Chinese used bronze and copper for the base of their work. The latter had sufficient reason for their choice of materials, as will be seen in a later chapter.

One of the most important chores, at least to the Western scholar, is the attempt to determine the approximate date a piece of Chinese art was created—whether it be a bronze vessel, a porcelain dish, or an item of enamel ware. Apparently, this problem carries much less weight with the Chinese themselves. Of all the art objects created by the Chinese, including paintings, pottery, and lacquer ware, pieces of enamel ware have proved the most difficult to date, even approximately. The usual custom of putting the artist's name and date or dynasty on an art object was rarely followed with respect to enamels. Where no mark of any kind is shown, various other means have been used to obtain a reasonable answer, such as comparing the design, materials, or colors with those of other art works having authentic identification. One of the most painstaking studies of this problem is contained in Sir Harry Garner's book.[10]

Cloisonné enamel ware made during the early days of the Ming dynasty has certain characteristics which distinguish it from later work. The base was usually much heavier, being of bronze and with gilded bronze cloisons. The design was comparatively simple and often done in the geometrical patterns so common in bronze work. The enamel was thicker, pits and blemishes were more common, and the colors more simple and intense. At the same time, an examination of those pieces of Ming ware which can be definitely identified as such will show that there are exceptions to every one of these general statements.

Therein lies the great puzzle of Chinese enamels; not even the mark or date can be blindly accepted as authentic. The most common "mark" of the Ming dynasty is that of the Ching T'ai period, 1450 to 1456. Yet it has been proved that the mark of Ching T'ai has been used as much as two hundred years later, probably in reverence for the excellence of the original. It should be noted that quite often the "copy" is as good as the original.

The manufacture of enamel ware—both in champlevé and

in cloisonné, along with other kinds of art—was greatly encouraged during the reign of K'ang Hsi (1662–1722) in the Ch'ing dynasty. In 1680, a glass factory was established in the royal palace at Peking, in which a great variety of glass articles was made. Much of the work was designed for and retained in the neighboring Buddhist temples. As compared with earlier work, the surface of the enamel was much more polished and less pitted, i.e., the pits were both fewer and smaller. The designs were more graceful and complex, the colors more varied but perhaps less intense. The base and cloisons were copper instead of bronze. The gilded bronze ornaments were the best in Chinese modeled art. The quality of the enamels made during this period and in the reigns of the two succeeding emperors, Yung Cheng (1723–1735) and Ch'ien Lung (1736–1795), is especially excellent.

For the student who would wish to learn more about the history of Chinese glass enamels than has been outlined here, numbers 6 and 10 of the Bibliography will be found to provide interesting and reliable information. Most of the best examples of enamel work, both champlevé and cloisonné, have long since been acquired by museums. At present, it seems to be out of fashion to display them.

The present volume is more concerned with the development of the art of enameling and the characteristics of the finished ware than in a discussion of the actual or estimated dates of production. It is well to keep in mind that purported age is only one factor —and not necessarily the most important—in the determination of the intrinsic value of a specimen. A thorough knowledge of these other factors will help to expose the common claim that a piece "is undoubtedly Ming," when it is obvious it was probably made a couple of centuries later. Stated differently, the general excellence in design, color, workmanship, and condition should be, to the average collector, of more importance than the date— unless the latter can be *proven*.

Coupled with the problem of date of manufacture is that of trying to determine when and how Chinese enameled ware first reached Europe. From the time of the travels of Marco Polo—

which were considered sheer fantasy for a century or so—ships from the West, mostly Spanish, Portuguese, and Italian, ventured farther and farther into the unknown East. They brought back with them an increasing amount of knowledge and greater quantities of goods, the most precious of the latter being silks, porcelain, and lacquers.

Porcelain, the most desirable of all, probably reached Europe early in the fifteenth century. From then on the demand for it and the secret of its making was exceedingly great, the two principal results being poor imitations and frustration. Among all the various skills and interests of China, enameled ware was considered a minor art, both in China and in the West. As a result there is little evidence that any appreciable amount of it reached Europe, directly or indirectly, before the nineteenth century—and then probably in connection with the importation of Chinese painted enamels, which will be discussed later.

CHAPTER IV

❧❧❧❧❧❧❧❧❧

Chinese Enamels: Methods of Creation

*W*ITH the comparatively recent revival (1950) in the decorative use of enamels, especially of Chinese and Japanese origin, there has been an increasing number of books—European and American—on the mechanics of this fascinating branch of art. These books are not so much interested in the history of enamels as they are in providing precise and reliable information on the design, materials, and creation of enameled ware, painted as well as the cloisonné type.

While the basic method has not changed in centuries, there are a number of improvements to encourage the modern craftsman. Instead of his having the laborious chore of preparing his own enamels, now carefully ground powders, in some two hundred colors, are easily available. Instead of having to hammer out the plate, dish, or cloisons himself, all these items may now be purchased. For firing, the old-time charcoal brazier has been replaced by the blast-torch and the electric kiln. The only items in short supply are the unique patience and technical ability of the Chinese and Japanese artist.

Glass enamels may be classified into three principal divisions: champlevé, cloisonné, and painted. As we have noted, the Chinese originally applied the term "fu-lin ware" or "falan" to the enameled ware first brought into China. The Japanese terms for the various types of enamels will be discussed later.

CHAMPLEVÉ ENAMELS

It appears that the earliest pieces of Chinese enameled ware were made by the champlevé process; there is a difference of opinion regarding this.

Because of the nature of the process, the base of an object to be finished in a champlevé design was usually cast bronze. For those parts of the vessel which were to be enameled, a design was drawn on the metal and then carved or chiseled to provide hollows into which the enamel paste was packed. The lines of the design—that is, the hollows or "pools"—did not touch. Those parts of the piece not to be enameled were either left plain or carved into a design similar to those done on ancient Chinese bronzes; these parts were usually gilded.

Having carefully packed the enamel paste, putting various colors into their respective pools, the next step was to fire the article and so fuse the paste into a glass enamel. The final steps were to grind and polish the enameled surface, using increasingly finer abrasives, until the desired finish was obtained.

Because of the difficulty of carving the bronze, the design was necessarily much more simple than could be obtained by the cloisonné method. For this reason, both methods were often combined in the same piece, according to the nature of the design. The more prominent parts of the design were done in champlevé; the finer lines were added in cloisonné. Examples of this kind of work can also be found in early German enameled ware—that is, prior to the fifteenth century.

Another characteristic peculiar to champlevé work is that, because the base was bronze (which contains tin), it was necessary to use opaque enamels; translucent enamels would have become opaque in the firing. The enamels used in the cloisonné portions were also opaque. In spite of this apparent limitation, the colors to be found in even the earliest ware of the Ming dynasty are brilliant and rated superior to those produced elsewhere. It should be noted that the heavy bronze base required for champlevé work did not need a counter-enamel on the back side of the metal—or interior of the vessel.

Although it is likely that the Chinese first learned about both champlevé and cloisonné enamels in the fourteenth century, their earliest work was done by the champlevé method. For fifteen centuries, the Chinese had molded or carved increasingly intricate and excellent designs into their bronze ware. The addition of colored vitreous enamels to portions of the design came as a natural variation. It should be noted that the boldness and character of the designs used in the ancient bronze ware were continued in the champlevé work for the next three centuries.

CLOISONNÉ ENAMELS

The most difficult step in the process of creating a piece of champlevé ware is excavating or gouging out the metal. In cloisonné work, the most important step is forming and placing the extremely fine ribbons which define the design. The narrow bands or ribbons which make the "fences" between colors are called cloisons; the material is usually the same as that in the base—copper, silver, or gold—although, as nearly as can be determined, bronze cloisons (on a bronze base) were most generally used during the Ming dynasty, that is, up to about the middle of the seventeenth century. Both in Chinese and in Japanese work, copper, bronze, and brass were sometimes used interchangeably for base and cloison; examples may also be found in which silver cloisons were used on a copper base.

The several steps required in the making of a piece of cloisonné enameled ware required a high degree of artistic and technical ability as well as great patience as can be seen from the following outline.

1. Design of the vessel and ornamentation. In many cases, the design has first been drawn and carefully colored by an experienced artist, on cloth or paper.

2. Cutting and forming the sheet metal—a step done by an

artisan skilled in shaping, welding, and polishing the required vessel.

3. Preparation of the various glass enamels, grinding them into fine powder form—each color kept in a separate dish.

4. The fine-line design is copied on the vessel with a brush and india ink.

5. The cloisons are carefully shaped to follow the intricate details of the design, and temporarily attached to the base or ground by the use of a rice or similar paste.

6. After the cloisons have been attached, the surface is dusted with a low-fusing solder and melted into place, replacing the temporary paste.

7. The powdered enamels, made into a paste with water, are placed in the individual cells or areas. The artist must know the final color desired, because the paste color, prior to the firing, bears no relation to it.

8. After giving the tightly packed paste time to dry, the article is fired, usually over an open charcoal fire. Because the enamel shrinks and may become pitted in the process of fusing, the process of filling the cells and firing must be repeated until the surface of the cell is up to or above the cloison.

9. The final step is careful grinding down of the enamel surface until the cloison design is revealed and the desired polish obtained. Corundum, sandstone, pumice powder, and charcoal are some of the abrasive agents used.

In the better examples of cloisonné ware, the exposed parts of the vessel and the cloisons were gilded, thus adding additional beauty and value to the work.

Exhibits illustrating the six principal steps in the manufacture of cloisonné enamel may be found in at least two museums: the Smithsonian Institution, Washington, D.C. and the Chicago Art Institute. However, at the present time, few or no Chinese or Japanese enamels are being displayed in the big city museums. A fortunate exception, already noted, is the permanent display in Springfield, Mass.[24]

Illustrations of the various steps in the creation of a piece of cloisonné enamel may be found in the following references: (a) A set of eight illustrations, *"Brooklyn Museum Quarterly,"* October, 1938, issue; (b) Six illustrations in the article, "The Art of True Enameling," *International Studio Magazine,* Vol. 16, March–June, 1902; (c) Six illustrations under the heading of "Enamel," *Encyclopedia Britannica.*

In China, the base or foundation for cloisonné enameling was generally copper, sometimes bronze or silver, rarely gold. The almost universal use of copper or bronze was because these two metals were held in much higher esteem in China than in other countries. More important was the fact that the enamel was found to cling to the metal as well as or better than to any other material. When silver was used, it presented special problems in the use of transparent or translucent enamels.

Available literature on the subject of cloisonné enamels gives little attention to the exact description of the metal used for the base—jar, bowl, vase, or box—and consequently there is some confusion in the use of the terms "bronze" and "brass." As now defined, brass is an alloy of copper and zinc; bronze is an alloy of copper and tin. Varying proportions of both tin and zinc were likely to be combined in the bronze used in the ancient bronze vessels, and the term "brass" has been used sometimes in the past although the metal was actually an alloy of copper and tin.

In contrast to brass, a piece of bronze is comparatively darker in color, thicker, and gives off a ring when tapped. The color depends largely on its age and condition, ranging from dull red toward a chocolate brown and, in more ancient work, even a bluish green. Bronze was always cast in its final form, except for any design chiseling, because it is far less malleable than brass. Bronze was found to hold the fused enamels better than brass.

Copper, even when it is not completely pure, is extremely malleable. It can be beaten and formed into the most intricate shapes, providing it is kept in a malleable state by frequent annealing. When a piece of sheet copper is being beaten into a desired shape, it becomes hard and stubborn to work. To return it to its originally malleable state, the metal is heated until red-hot, then dropped into cold water. Copper is always an Indian red; brass is much more yellowish—gold colored—due to the presence of zinc in its composition.

Even after close inspection, it is often difficult to determine the exact kind of material used in the body of the article, either for champlevé or cloisonné ware. A piece of cloisonné enamel having a copper base is always much lighter in weight than a vessel made of bronze; if tapped with a finger, the copper gives off only a dull ring as compared with the bell-like tone of bronze. Although the back side or inside of an article made of bronze was not enameled, all exposed parts—such as handles, ornaments, and the lines of the design—were gilded. When thin copper was used as the base (as in almost all cloisonné work), it was found necessary to "counter-enamel" the back side or interior. This added step was taken in order to stiffen the metal and to prevent the enamel from cracking—a factor which also explains why so much of the Chinese enamel-on-copper has a brass or bronze rim and bottom. This latter embellishment not only protects the edges of the cloisonné but adds considerably to the appearance of the finished product.

Copper, brass, and bronze melt at temperatures between 1750° and 1981° Fahrenheit. Fine silver contains less copper than sterling silver and melts at 1760°. The melting point of ordinary glass ranges from 1800° to 2900°, depending on the ingredients. Medium fusing enamels melt at from 1450° to 1550°. When the cloisons are soldered to the base, the solder must have a relatively high melting point; the average silver solder has a melting point of 1335°. It is therefore essential that only appropriate types of glass enamels be used, having the same characteristics as the base, in order to expand and contract at about the same rate under different heat conditions.

One of the most amazing features in a piece of cloisonné ware is the meticulous artistry shown in the design and placing of the cloisons or fillets. Although the principal purpose of the ribbons is to serve as a fence or partition between the various colors in the

design, a ribbon is often used to represent a wandering tendril, the
veins of a leaf, or a background scroll. That is, the cloison does not
always serve to separate two colors but may cut through the same-
color background.

In the earliest Chinese enamels, at least during the Ming period, the cloisons were made of the same material as the base,
usually bronze. Close examination shows that they are of varying
thickness, indicating that they were undoubtedly made by the tedious process of pounding out the individual strips by hand. In
later work, the metal ribbons were made either by drawing the
metal through a die, or cutting them from a thin sheet of the desired material; this latter method allowed a wide degree of fineness
in width and thickness. There is evidence to indicate that solder
—lead or silver—was not always used, especially in later
Chinese and much of the Japanese work. Instead, a vegetable glue,
with the help of the glass paste, was employed to hold the cloisons
in place until the enamel was fired.

Specimens of the various vitreous enamels were retained in
solid form to provide an accurate index to the final effect desired;
the portion which was ground into the fine-powder paste lost all
color relation to the solid color until it was fired when it returned
to its former state. Even a change in firing, such as the degree of
heat or the amount of air around the object, could affect the final
result. In spite of these requirements, it is generally agreed that the
enamels of the Ming dynasty had a purity and depth of color un-
equaled in later work.

Each color of enamel paste was kept in a separate saucer and
applied, at least in early Chinese ware, as a single color in a cell. In
later work, a cell was "shaded" by the use of two colors, sometimes kept separate, sometimes mixed. A bamboo pen or small stylet was used to pack the paste tightly into its predetermined area.

Although the firing was probably done over a small charcoal
fire, with or without some form of hood or baffle to keep the heat
as uniform as possible, it required only a short time as compared
with the firing of a ceramic piece. Because of the shrinking of the
enamel and a certain amount of pitting—due to the uneven

packing of the paste and the failure to remove air bubbles—it was often found necessary to repeat the process of packing and firing, until the enamels completely filled the cloisons.

There appears to be a decided difference of opinion as to the loss of artistic value due to the "pinhole" pitting of the enamels. It is generally agreed that the pitting was not too objectionable but served as an aid in the determination of the probable age, later work being almost devoid of this characteristic. It is argued that repeated firings—especially to remove the pitting—often affected the purity and brilliance of the colors, even to the point of their becoming muddy.

A subdivision under cloisonné enamels is called "filigree." In this type of work, the principal difference is that each cell is only partly filled with enamel and acquires only a "fire polish"— meaning it has a duller polish than when the usual procedure is used. In a variation of this method, only the design itself is filled with the colored enamels; the background is the bare metal of the base—usually bronze. The unique design and workmanship indicate Chinese origin. This is another example of the general lack of reliable information or of accuracy in the material that is available.

PAINTED ENAMELS

In addition to the decoration of metal objects by either the champlevé or cloisonné process, the Chinese also produced large quantities of painted enamels, but did not take up this type of art for some three hundred years after its first work with the two above-named categories. Trade, both by sea and by land greatly increased during the period from the seventeenth to the nineteenth century, the result of the increased demand by the European countries for the strange and beautiful arts of China, especially porcelain and silk.

Porcelain with polychrome decoration *—far surpassing anything produced in the West—had been made since the middle of

* Background: Polychrome porcelain vs. Canton painted metal.

the Ming dynasty. Because of the excellence and the comparative cheapness of the Chinese work, various European countries, such as France, England, and Holland, began the practice of taking ceramic ware to China either to have it decorated or copied in the European fashion. The decoration was in the form of coats of arms, portraits, scenery, and for various kinds of table service, using the foreign designs brought to the Chinese artisans. Period accounts indicate that the superior skill of execution and the comparative cheapness of the work were contributing factors in having this kind of work done several thousand miles from its eventual destination.

Porcelain—whether plain, glazed, or polychrome decorated—was entirely developed in China, centuries earlier than any foreign product. On the other hand, enamel painting originated in France and England and was called "foreign porcelain" by the Chinese, due to its resemblance to Chinese porcelains. It was apparently not before the eighteenth century that the Chinese began the production of painted enamels, with Canton becoming the center of this type of work, hence the term "Canton enamels." In this type of work, the base was usually copper. After the base—dish, teapot, etc.—is completed, it is first given a coat of enamel, usually white. The design is then drawn on it and *painted* with the same vitreous enamels used in cloisonné and champlevé work. The resulting appearance is similar to but not as brilliant or polished as that done by the two previous methods.

It is interesting to note that, because of the resemblance to champlevé or cloisonné ware, a piece of painted enamel (with its typical Chinese design) may be offered for sale as "genuine" cloisonné. However, to confuse the collector, there are good examples of combined painted and cloisonné enamel on the same piece. In this type of work, the panels or medallions may be painted, while the surrounding background is done in cloisonné.

CHAPTER V

<figure>ornamental divider</figure>

Chinese Enamels: Design and Symbolism

*I*N *THE FIELD* of imaginative and decorative design and symbolism, the Chinese artists have never been surpassed. An ancient rule in Chinese art was called "rhythmic vitality," meaning a quest for harmony and rightness regardless of medium. This rare combination of artistic sense and technical skill is equally notable, whether the object be a bronze pot, a piece of carved jade, a porcelain bowl, or an embroidered silken robe. The statement may be easily proven if an item of Chinese art, in any medium, is compared with one of a similar category, as produced in the same era in any European country.

As to the much discussed subject of the derivation of the various art motifs used in Chinese art, it is generally agreed that the small proportion of designs and symbols which may have been brought into the country (from Arabia, Egypt, Byzantium, or the Roman Empire) soon acquired a typically oriental stylization all its own—one as diverse as the Chinese imagination.

From the time of the earliest Chinese bronzes, first made some four thousand years ago, the decoration has been symbolic and the symbols decorative. A clear and concise account—both in words and pictures—of the design and symbolism in these bronzes, may be found in Vol. 1 of Dr. Bushell's *Chinese Art.*[6] For example, during the Hsia dynasty, some 2000 years B.C., the emperor ordered a set of bronze tripod caldrons, to be carved with maps and figures illustrating the natural products of the provinces. They were to show representations of the evil spirits of the storm and the malignant demons of the woods and wild places, so that the common people might recognize and avoid them.

A study of the decoration to be found in primitive Chinese bronzes is of value if one is to understand and appreciate the symbolism brought down through the centuries to the decoration of enamels. The original motif may be repeated to make an over-all pattern, simple or complex, symmetrical or not; one of the most common is a rectangular scroll, so frequently found on Greek or Etruscan pottery. This similarity of design does not necessarily indicate possible commerce between one country and another so long ago.

The second, and just as important, type of design depicts the animal world, in which the Chinese imagination has always excelled that of any other race. The endless variety of this category, which has been called a "mythological zoology," includes dragons, phoenixes, and assorted fearsome monsters such as the ogre. This fantasia of strange beings is so cleverly woven into the design as to be overlooked by the casual observer. An odd circle may represent an ogre's eye, or a modified yang-yin symbol. A meandering line through the design may be a fanciful interpretation of the symbolic pondweed or "china grass"; a series of half-circles may represent ocean waves; an indented lozenge, a prunus blossom. Often the color may help to identify the symbol; every part of the design has a meaning all its own. It is a tribute to the distinctive attributes of Chinese art, regardless of the medium used, that so many writers have been impelled to search for such descriptive expressions as *sensitive design, tranquillity, subtle colors, timeless serenity*. No one yet has devised a yardstick by which to measure what are commonly called the "aesthetic values" of this uniquely Chinese phantasma.

Primitive nature worship existed in China back some 3000 to 4000 years B.C., as evidenced in Chinese traditions and arts. The Emperor Wen, first of the Chou dynasty (twelfth century B.C.), had a collection of animals he called "The Garden of Intelligence." Just how important a part mysterious symbolism played is illustrated by a legend relating to the making of ancient bronze vessels, especially the type used in religious ceremonies. Because the bronze was supposed to embody the yang-yin—the male and female Dual Principle—the bronze caster and his wife were compelled to throw themselves into the molten metal. Later, it was decreed that, since the furnace itself embodied the male spirit, only the wife was needed to guarantee an acceptable mixture.

By the time of the Han dynasty (206 B.C. to A.D. 220), a complicated but precise cosmic order had been evolved, which may be briefly outlined as follows: The Vault of Heaven was divided into Four Quadrants—North, East, South, and West. These quadrants corresponded to the Four Seasons—Winter, Spring, Summer, and Fall. Presiding over the Four Quadrants and the Four Seasons were the Four Supernatural Beings: Tortoise (or Turtle), Dragon, Phoenix, and Tiger (or Unicorn). In turn, these symbolized the four classes into which all animals were divided: shell-covered, scaly, feathered, and hairy creatures. In addition, there were the Four Elements: Water, Wood, Fire, and Metal: also the Four Colors: Black, Green (or Blue), Red, and White. Certain flowers also symbolized the four seasons.

So, as set forth in the ancient Chinese text, the full relationship for the four groups was as follows:

Turtle	North	Winter	Black	Water	Prune Blossom
Dragon	East	Spring	Green	Wood	Tree Peony
Phoenix	South	Summer	Red	Fire	Lotus Blossom
Tiger	West	Fall	White	Metal	Chrysanthemum

There was a fifth Cardinal Point or Primordial Element: the Center of the Universe. It represented the Emperor and its color was Yellow. In certain kinds of ceramic ware made during the Han dynasty, the mythological figures representing the Four Quadrants of the Chinese Heaven were all depicted: Black Tortoise of the North; Green (or blue) Dragon of the East; Phoenix (or Red Bird) of the South; White Tiger of the West.

From ancient times, the Chinese—meaning those peoples who first occupied the general territory of the Yellow and Yangtze river basins—believed that earthly order corresponded to a universal heavenly or cosmic order and was dependent on it.

In order to explain the theory of the Universe—the mysterious ways in which it operated and the forces of Nature, both celestial and terrestrial—there was evolved the concept of Yang and Yin, the Dual Principle. The Yang-Yin symbol (sometimes written Yin-Yang) is in the form of a circle having a sinuous *S* drawn through the center to divide it into two equal comma-shaped parts, always shown in contrasting colors. Yang represents Heaven, Sun, Male, Activity, Light, Strength, Warmth, Dryness, and odd numbers, the north side of a river, and the south side of a hill. Yin was just the opposite; it represented Earth, Moon, Female, Passivity, Darkness, Weakness, Cold, and even numbers, the south bank of a river, and the north side of a hill. The symbols for Yang were the Dragon and the Phoenix; for Yin, the Turtle and the Tiger. See *Chinese Art Symbols,* by W. H. Hawley.[14]

With the exception of Heaven (purely Yang) and Earth (purely Yin), all things are composed of both characteristics in unequal proportions. It is the balance between these two forces which constitutes the order of the universe. It was more than a balance; it was the periodic changes which took place between them, such as light and dark, or the changing seasons. Here was an explanation of seasonal changes: in Spring the Dragon ascends into the sky; in Autumn he returns to Earth, perhaps to the river from which he came. A similar principle held for each of the other phenomena of nature.

Closely related to the conception of Yang-Yin is that of the Eight Trigrams (Pa Kua), each a three-line symbol, which represented the eight spheres of the universe. With the passage of time, they were expanded into sixty-four hexagrams. Soothsayers used these symbols as a code by which to observe natural phenomena, consult the ancestral spirits, and so interpret the will of Heaven. The derivation of this principle is in itself a legend: an ancient Chinese sovereign was standing on the bank of the Yellow River one day when he saw a horse-like dragon emerge from the water. On the back of the dragon were certain mystic signs which the Emperor copied and later evolved into the Eight Trigrams.

The eight spheres of the Universe included the essence of everything which existed in it; the visible world of Nature corresponded to the invisible in every way. In these spheres, all things were related to each other on a sexual principle; that is, the two types of symbols represented male and female, similar to the Yang-Yin theory. The two principles—Heaven and Earth—were also divided in the other six, unequally but in certain definite ratios.

The Eight Trigrams were usually grouped in the form of an octagon, around the Yang-Yin symbol; the unit became a feature in various kinds of art and was symbolic of an harmonious universe. The first symbol—Heaven and Male—was represented by three short, solid lines in three rows. Earth and Female were represented by three dashed lines, in three rows. The remaining six symbols—Water, Fire, Wind, Thunder, Vapor, and Mountains —were shown by three-line combinations of solid and dashed lines.

In addition to the symbolism attached to Yang-Yin and the Eight Trigrams, other phenomena of nature became animated with spirit inhabitants and represented in spirit form. These symbols were many and in many forms: animal, bird, flower, a household object, an abstract drawing. Only the most important and the most common can be described here. For a more complete list, Hawley's illustrated charts [14,15] will be found to be most interesting.

DRAGON

The dragon is one of the most ancient of Chinese symbols, a creature which appears in every branch of Chinese art, sometimes stylized to a degree which may resemble little more than a character in Chinese writing. It is probably the most hybridized animal that human imagination ever produced: it may have the head of a camel or a snake; a cow's ears; a deer's horns; whiskers and a beard; various types of body; a carp's scales; the tail of an alligator or snake (forked at the end in a special three-part tip); and a hawk's claws.

The number of claws has been a matter of dispute, in that an ordinary Chinese dragon was once supposed to have four claws, while an Imperial dragon had five claws. In contrast to this, the Japanese dragon has only three claws. There seem to be enough exceptions to indicate that either there was no strict rule, or the rule may have changed with the centuries.

The dragon was originally thought of as friendly, regardless of how fearful it may have looked, representing as it did a beneficial force of nature. Eventually, the dragon became the emblem of the Emperor himself. Although the dragon lived in a river or the sea, it ascended into the clouds in spring, to bring welcome rains and fertile fields. It was believed that a thunderstorm was nothing more than two dragons fighting in the sky. There were, however, a few species of dragons which were fierce and cruel, but there were ways of telling one of these from a good dragon.

One Chinese dragon was known to have 117 scales with the power to do good and 36 scales which could do harm. While green or blue was the prescribed color of a dragon, it eventually came in a color best suited to the design and the imagination of the artist. Quite often, he is shown with a design of flames (usually red) around him and perhaps close by a "pearl" with flames around it.

The dragon had a range of magical powers as wide as the universe. The Chinese even attributed a part of this power to the artists who drew them. In the fifth century of the Christian era, there lived a great painter who exhibited a wall painting or mural of four dragons, all without eyes. Asked why, he explained that it might be dangerous to give sight to such fierce creatures. Finally, to quiet his critics, he painted eyes on two of the dragons; whereupon, so the legend goes, the wall broke down, the air was filled with thunder and lightning, and the two dragons took off on clouds into the sky. The dragons without eyes remained behind.

Ancient Egypt, Chaldea, and various countries of Europe had dragons as a part of their mythology. They usually had wings, had the shape of a snake or a lizard, breathed fire and were symbolic of sin, paganism, and evil powers. The Chinese conception was different; the dragon could fly, although it had no wings; it always had four feet; it was usually a friendly creature. Even though it may have been depicted as having the head and ears of a wolf, the horns of a goat, and a "rat's tail" from each side of the nose, it was regarded as a deified force of Nature by the Chinese.

PHOENIX

The Dragon and the Phoenix are Yang creatures and are used in decorative work much more than the two Yin animals, the Tiger and the Tortoise. The Phoenix bird is also common, in one form or another, to Egyptian and Arabian as well as Chinese mythology. At first, according to Dr. Bushell, it was depicted as a gigantic eagle, similar to the imaginary and fanciful bird of ancient India, Persia, and Greece. In Arabia, it was fabled to live 500 to 1000 years, then by its own act to be consumed by fire, to arise again in youthful freshness from the ashes.

By the time of the Han dynasty, the phoenix had become a native of China in its conception. A fabulous bird of no particular species, it became the subject of many legends, many designs, and the mysterious center of endless discussion. It was sometimes called the Red Bird. The Chinese imagination hatched a combination of peacock, pheasant, crane, and the local rooster. As usually depicted in paintings, silks, and other media, it had a medium-size head and beak, one or two graceful plumes curling from the top of the head, an arched neck, and a very long tail of three gracefully waving-plumes. With the passing of time, it became more colorful, its claws less conspicuous, and was always shown in flight.

The Phoenix was the symbol for Beauty, Goodness, Prosperity, Peace, and eventually the personal emblem of the Empress of China. Although the phoenix may be found in Chinese sculpture and in its bronzes, it is seldom shown in its enamel work, that is, not as much as the more popular dragon. In Japanese enamels, a similar bird is a popular part of the design.

OGRE OR DEVIL MASK

Unlike the dragon, the Ogre was always as mean as he looks, about the worst of all the fantastic creatures of ancient mythology. Although considered to be a product of the Byzantine imagination, a similar mask may be found in the ancient art of such diverse peoples as the Mayan Indians and the Scandinavians.

The Ogre is usually depicted as a mask, sometimes as two serpents in profile facing each other, so as to form a full-face mask looking somewhat like a horned bull or fabulous monster. The mask was often so stylized that it became a part of a geometric pattern, whether the work be done in bronze or other medium. However, both in bronze and later in cloisonné enamels, it was often carved in the round—as a part of a handle, foot, or ornament. It was usually portrayed with two enormous eyes and powerful jaws, ". . . the better to eat you with." As might be expected, it was the symbol for Gluttony and Avarice. Either in the flat or in the round, only the head was shown.

LION

It has been difficult to learn the place the lion holds in the symbolism of the Chinese. Stone carvings, dating back to the sixth century, suggest that it had something to do with Buddhism, as a "Defender of the law." The Buddhist religion was first officially recognized in China in A.D. 67. At one time, the lion is supposed to have existed in India but not in China.

Quite often, either in the form of a lion or a close member of the chimera family, it was carved in heroic proportions to stand guard before the tomb of a prince or an emperor. The usual Chinese lion, also known as a "fu-lion" or "shih," appears to be made up of three parts: one part lion, one part pekinese dog, and one part monster with a Chinese accent. In enamel work, it is cast in the round, in gilded bronze, and its favorite position is to stand—or sometimes sit—on guard on the top of an ornate censer or incense burner. Sometimes, it was itself the incense burner; as such, it was known as a "tai chih" or monster lion.

OTHER ANIMALS AND BIRDS

Many other animals appear in one form or another in Chinese art, but rarely in enamel work. Among them are the following: horse, elephant, tiger, unicorn, monkey, dog, cat, hare, cock, and deer. Birds include the crane, bat, pheasant, and a variety of ducks.

The butterfly is often used in one form or another of the various arts, partly because of its ornamental design, partly because it is a symbol of conjugal felicity and joy. A pair of fishes is symbolic of marriage, fertility, and conjugal felicity.

FLOWERS

In China, flowers have always played a prominent part in the religious and decorative arts of the country, some of them dating back to primitive times. There was not only a flower which was emblematic for each of the four seasons, there was one for each month of the year—although the latter may not have been the same in the different parts of China. The following list is the one usually accepted:

1. January (Winter): Prunus or Prune blossom
2. February: Peach blossom—Charm against Evil
3. March (Spring): Tree Peony—Riches, Honor
4. April: Cherry blossom (double)—Feminine Beauty
5. May: Magnolia—Feminine Sweetness
6. June: Pomegranate (carnation-like flower)
7. July (Summer): Lotus blossom—Creative Power, Purity
8. August: Pear blossom (five petals)—Wise Administration

9. September: Mallow (single blossom)
10. October (Autumn): Chrysanthemum—Joviality, Life of Ease
11. November: Gardenia (double blossom)
12. December: Poppy

Prunus, the January flower, may be translated as Prune, Plum, Peach, or Cherry—all members of the same species; here it is usually the Plum blossom. Another Prunus, the Cherry blossom (April) is depicted as either single or double. Extensive use is made of most of the above flowers, often in extremely stylized form—especially in painting and enameling. In later years, these flowers are to be found in great profusion on the silken robes of the Emperor and his court.

PONDWEED

Often found wandering among the larger figures—mostly in enameled ware—is a vine-like design known as Pondweed or Waterweed; the Japanese call it "China Grass." Sometimes its alternate leaves make it look quite realistic; other times, its curling, constantly branching contour is formed by two parallel cloisons, in colors different from those used in the background.

CLOUDS, WAVES, AND FLAMES

In much of the Chinese art—especially enameled work—depicting a dragon, the design includes various combinations of clouds, waves, and flames serving as a background; they were intended to be both symbolic and decorative. The waves are drawn in various forms: overlapping, inverted, half-circles, sometimes quite realistic breakers; they represent the dragon's part-time river abode.

When the dragon ascended into the sky it was surrounded by clouds, whether the work was done in bronze, enamels, or in silken robes. In enamel work, the clouds were often in the form of an irregular-shaped heart, outlined in double cloisons. The colors within the double cloisons were different from those in the surrounding background. The remainder of the ground was filled with single-cloison clouds.

Blood-red streaming flames often accompany a dragon, either belching from his jaws or swirling through the air around him. Aside from the fact that they help to give him character and prestige, little explanation has been found for their presence.

SPIRALS AND SCROLLS

The subject of spirals and scrolls in Chinese design is another instance of little explanation in available records. These minor decorative devices appear in an endless variety of styles and their use dates back two thousand years and more; they were often used in addition to waves and clouds in the design of bronzes and enamels.

A spiral of many turns, usually in a square pattern, is to be found on ancient bronzes. Later, it was depicted as a variety of curl—a simple C, especially in enamels. The tiny curls are powdered over the ground, like stars scattered in the sky. Beginning with the ancient bronzes, the spiral was extended into a continuous band or scroll and was known as the "thunder scroll." A twisting ribbon was called the "cloud scroll." This kind of decoration—in stone and in bronze—took many forms, from a straight line, incised or fluted, to a wavy series of lines and on to a more complex treatment.

As usual, when there is a blank space in the art records, there has been speculation as to the purpose and significance in the use of such ornamental detail as the spiral and scroll. One writer wonders about the symbolism involved. Is it important to know why an artist has blended the symbolic with the decorative? Another writer is of the opinion that the Chinese artist just did not like a blank space anywhere in the particular type of art he produced; therefore he filled the ground with spirals and scrolls, or perhaps clouds. In the art of enameling, it has been contended that the artisan would have invited trouble if he had failed to provide a close network of cloisons to support the enamel. However, there are any number of examples of cloisonné enamels, especially Japanese, in which the design and the cloisons occupy only a small part of the total space; the greater part of the surface is completely bare of cloisons and shows no ill effects of any kind. This type of enamel work is still being made at the present time, without soldered cloisons, in such centers of production as Kyoto and Nagoya, Japan.

In addition to the above described designs and decorations, it should be mentioned that various script characters—denoting good fortune to the possessor—are often blended into the design of enamels, silken robes, and the like.

CHAPTER VI

※⟨⟨⟨⟨⟨⟨⟨⟨⟨⟩⟩⟩⟩⟩⟩⟩⟩⟩※

Chinese Enamels: The Conquest of Color

A MAGNIFYING-GLASS examination of the color and gemlike quality of the various kinds of Chinese and Japanese enamels, even in the less desirable specimens, cannot help but impress the viewer with the centuries of patient technical experimentation which must have been required to produce them. Although it is generally agreed that the Chinese had known about glass, from imports dating back to the beginning of the Christian era, it was not until about the fifth century that they first began to make glass objects from local materials. They eventually excelled, in quality and color, anything brought from the West. From the first, the principle seems to have been to produce glass whose color should match amethyst, lapis lazuli, jade, and other semi-precious gem stones, including rock crystal or quartz—even though the Chinese used opaque enamels much more than the translucent kind.

With a thousand years and more of experience in painting and similar arts, such as embroidered silks, the Chinese had developed much knowledge and a subtle sense of color. It helps to explain why, as previously quoted from the book *Ko ku yao lun,* enameled ware was considered "only fit for use in the ladies' inner apartments, being too gaudy for the libraries of scholars of simple tastes."

As explained in a previous chapter, most enamels look completely different in powdered form and when fired, so that the artisan must know the exact effect and color he wants each time he applies a bit of paste. A new hue or color cannot be produced merely by mixing two enamels in powder form. Each color is composed of a different proportion of flux and the coloring oxide—and often produced under different firing conditions.

In the process of learning to make colored glass, the ancient craftsmen of the Mediterranean region found that they could make a cobalt-blue glass as a substitute for the semi-precious lapis lazuli; an opaque bluish-green glass as a good imitation of turquoise; a reddish-brown glass to take the place of carnelian or garnet. How much of this knowledge and experience in the coloring of glass was carried into China is not known. The colors found in early Chinese-made glass were probably due to the chance use of available native oxides, rather than to a desire for a certain result.

For example, a deep purplish-blue was obtained from a combination of cobalt and manganese silicates; a rich green was derived from copper silicate; the so-called "imperial yellow" (egg-yolk yellow) required the use of antimony. If copper was mixed with a deoxidizing flux, a brilliant blood-red (*sang de boeuf*) resulted, but a soft turquoise blue could be obtained with the same combination fused in the presence of excess niter.

The Chinese artisan's knowledge of the effect produced by the use of a specific oxide to produce a specific color in glassware was carried on to the new arts of producing ceramic and glass-enameled ware. The making and decorating of porcelain had been a part of Chinese art for several centuries prior to the inception of creating enamel wares. By the nature of the process, there was not as much freedom, in design and coloring, allowed in the latter as was enjoyed by the porcelain painter.

The following excerpt from Dr. Bushell's treatise on enamels [6] provides a concise description of the colors to be found in the enameled ware made during the Ming dynasty, but should be compared with similar material contained in Sir Harry Garner's book.[10]

> There are two well contrasted shades of blue, a dark blue of lapis-lazuli tone without the dulness of washing blue, and a pale sky-blue with the slightest tinge of green. The red is of dark coral tint rather than brickdust, the yellow full-bodied and pure. Greens

derived from copper are sparingly used, *rouges d'or* are entirely absent from their scheme of decoration. Black and white give the worst results, the former fails in depth and lustre, the latter is generally cloudy and muddy.

With the passing of time, Chinese colors became less vivid, more subtle in relation to each other, with less pitting in the surface of the enamels. Sir Harry Garner made use of this slowly changing appearance in the enamels he studied as a valuable index to the probable date of manufacture. He reports in effect as follows: During the fifteenth century, the colors were simple, rarely two in a cell: turquois blue (invariably used for the background), cobalt (dark) blue, dark green, red, yellow, and white. By the sixteenth century, there was greater variety: yellow and green occupying the same cell, a somewhat translucent purple, a dull blue replacing the cobalt blue, red, yellow, a half-translucent brown, and a so-called "Ming pink" which was really a mixture of red and white.

When two colors were first used in the same cell, they were kept apart, except that they may have fused together to some extent in the firing. Later, the colors were mixed more minutely until the identity of the individual colors was lost. The turquoise blue became a turquoise green. Still later, as many as three colors were used in the same cell.

About the same range of colors was used in the seventeenth century, but somewhat paler and with the addition of a dark grayish hue. The famous rose-pink, derived from gold, did not come into use until about the beginning of the eighteenth century.

The importance of color to the student or collector of enameled ware cannot be stressed too much. It is often a more dependable index to age and value than design or workmanship. The most logical course to follow in order to distinguish between fact and fiction is to "memorize" the individual colors used in accredited specimens. This may be done in two ways: examination in a museum such as the diversified and excellent exhibit at Springfield, Mass.,[24] or by a close study of the realistic color-photographs contained in such books as the one by Sir Harry Garner.[10]

This discussion of the changing use of color is of interest principally because other means of identification of the age and intrinsic value of a specimen may be either misleading or entirely lacking—a field in which there are no answers, at least at present.

Vase, Japanese, four and one-eighth inches high with silver cloisons on porcelain. Rare example of work signed by Namikama.

ABOVE: Pear-shaped copper teapot, Japanese, four inches high.
Ho-ho birds with brown background and gold sparkle.

RIGHT: Plate, Japanese, six inches
in diameter. Copper cloisons on
copper. Tree peony on brown
ground with gold sparkle.

CHAPTER VII

※⚛⚛⚛⚛⚛⚛⚛⚛⚛⚛⚛⚛※

Chinese Enamels in Relation to Other Arts of China

A CHAPTER on the related arts of China should prove helpful to an appreciation of the work done in enamels. Most of the literature of China pertains to those other fields of art in which it has always held a unique position in the world: bronzes, pottery, tomb figures, silks, lacquers, porcelain, ivory carvings, and painting. For much of the work done in these other media, the details of date, artist, origin, are noted either on the item itself or carefully described in current Chinese records. These sources are valuable as a means by which to learn similar facts relating to Chinese enameled ware.

Sometimes the design or symbolism used, or the peculiarities of color, suggest age and origin. The colors used in making champlevé and cloisonné enamels during the Ming dynasty are similar to those shown on the painted porcelains of that period. The symbolism woven into the brocades and silks of any period may be found repeated in the enamels being made. There are, however, differences in the conception and treatment of design and subject in one branch of art as compared with another. For example, human figures often appear in painting, pottery, lacquer work, and carved ivories—but rarely in bronzes or in enamel wares.

Regardless of the medium used, the Chinese artist developed a style peculiar to each, which has had many diverse imitators—a fact the collector should always keep in mind. The search for authenticity and the endless argument regarding identification can be overdone. This precept has been well stated in the book *Aspects of Chinese Painting*, by Mr. Alan Priest, Curator of Far Eastern Art, Metropolitan Art Museum, New York City. In a discussion of a certain painting, he says:

> Squabble about its authenticity, squabble about its date, he who chooses may. Whether this picture actually was painted by Chao Po-chu or not I do not know, but I am convinced it is of his period, the Sung dynasty. And even suppose that the blasphemous suggestion that it could be the work of a 19th century snuff bottle painter should be proved . . . what then? No talk, pontifical or irresponsible, can alter the intrinsic loveliness of this little picture. . . .

The above statement is even more applicable to the category of enameled wares, for reasons already discussed. That is, a knowledge of those branches of Chinese art, in which dates and ages can be reasonably ascertained, cannot help but give assurance to the buyer or collector of enameled wares of their intrinsic value.

CERAMICS—POTTERY AND PORCELAIN

Before discussing the various details of this branch of art, it is necessary to define the terms used. Ceramics (from a Greek word meaning "earthenware") covers the history and art of making pottery. While pottery may be defined as including any object made of clay and fired—even tiles and bricks—the acceptable use of the term limits it to utensils and vessels. Porcelain is a special kind of earthenware, containing ingredients other than clay. The universal use of clay, even from prehistoric times, is due to the great ease with which it can be molded and its extreme hardness when dried, either by the sun or by fire.

The ancient Chinese word for pottery is "t'ao," a term meaning "kiln" but which was applied to all kinds of ware fired in a kiln. Later, the term became "yao," which also meant kiln and the ware fired in it. Whether the ware be called earthenware, pottery, stoneware, or porcelain, it is all derived from clay; the distinguishing characteristic is the temperature at which each kind must be fired. Earthenware remains porous because it can stand only a comparatively low degree of firing—about 1450° Fahrenheit. By contrast, certain types of hard porcelain require as much as 2600°.

In order to raise the temperature to the melting point of clay and at the same time prevent breaking the vessel, it is necessary to add to the clay a varying amount of silica in some form (sand, powdered quartz, or even powdered potsherds). This mixture requires a relatively high degree of heat but the resulting ware will be as impermeable as stone and is usually called "gres" or stoneware. The action of fire on ordinary clay is to give it a brown color, due to the presence of iron, although it may result in almost any color as there are wide variations in the composition of the clay. This first firing goes by the name of the "body" of the vessel, to distinguish it from any over-coats which may be added.

Common white clay, so called because it remains white even after firing, is not malleable enough to be formed into vessels of itself, but is used in a fluid condition as a "slip" or wash. Another coating, a "glaze," is usually added over the slip. The glaze may be applied to make the vessel less permeable to liquids, or as decoration on ware which is of itself impermeable. Glazes were of various kinds, depending on the nature of the base, the firing temperature, and the result desired: alkaline (lime, potash, magnesia), the lead type, and the vitreous type (like those used on metal enameled ware, as cloisonné.

Porcelain is a translucent type of pottery, often called "china" because it was first developed in China and manufactured for many centuries in that country before other countries were able to learn the secrets of its ingredients and making. The Chinese first refer to porcelain under the name of "tz'u," as early as the Han dynasty; it was defined as a hard, compact, fine-grained, translucent pottery, giving a clear musical note when struck. Other references state that a type of true porcelain was first produced sometime between the Han and the T'ang dynasties. There are two principal types of porcelain: hard paste, containing only the natural elements, kaolin and petuntse; soft paste, never made in China, in which frit (glass) is used as a substitute for the natural stone.

During the T'ang and Sung dynasties, the manufacture of porcelain reached an ever-increasing state of perfection—a goal never equaled by any other country at any time. To appreciate the significance of this statement, Chinese arts during this period (from the sixth century to the twelfth) should be compared with the general level of civilization existing in the rest of the world. It was nearly a thousand years from the time of the first development of porcelain in China until samples of it reached Europe, probably in the fifteenth century. It was another two centuries or so before any of the Western countries was able to make anything approaching true porcelain.

As nearly as can be learned from the small amount of early Chinese literature on the subject, porcelain was first made at Ching-te-chen on the Yangtze River, because of the large deposits of the basic materials to be found there. Petuntse, or china stone, provided a glass-like flux which was added to the white clay (kaolin); the mixture became the body of all porcelain. Kaolin was also used, centuries ago, as a remedy for gastric complaints; it can still be bought in some apothecary shops.

The glaze used in Chinese porcelain making was also ground petuntse, mixed with lime to increase its fusibility. The best pieces of petuntse, selected for their greenish hue, were reserved for this purpose; the lime also helped to give the glaze the characteristic tinge of green or blue.

During the Sung dynasty, the glazes were in shades of white, in bluish or purplish grays, in green—from pale sea-green, "celadon," to deep olive—in browns from light chamois to shades approaching black, and in bright red or dark purple. Especially notable are the hues of pale purple—often splashed with red, brilliant grass-green or onion green, a pale gray-blue, and a deep purple or aubergine. In some cases, a mottled effect was obtained. Probably the most famous color was cobalt blue, said to have been brought to China from Arabia. The earliest "blue-and-white" porcelain was made in the Sung dynasty, became popular during the Ming dynasty and was exported in large quantities.

The glaze may be applied in any one of three ways: by dipping the vessel in a water-solution containing the desired mineral colors; applying with a brush; or blowing onto the vessel by use of a tube covered with a thin gauze to serve as an atomizer. The Chinese applied the glaze to the raw body and then fired it, a process which created a much better result than that used by Western countries, in which the glaze was applied to the (fired) biscuit.

The color of the particular glaze depends on the characteristics of the metal oxide used: copper gave a wide range of reds; iron produced beautiful yellows, browns, or blacks—depending on firing conditions; manganese gave delicate shades of peacock blue, violet, and purple. During the sixteenth century, a dark blue of marvellous depth and luster was used as a glaze. Also, during the Ming dynasty, the vitreous colors used in champlevé and cloisonné enameling were extensively used in the decoration of porcelain, with results beyond comparison.

The glazes used during the K'ang Hsi dynasty (1662–1722) were copper-red and maroon, fading into "peach-bloom" shades. The more intense colors of earlier periods were succeeded by softer hues. Other colors, known as crushed strawberry, apple green, and peach blossom were developed. It was not until the eighteenth century that tones of color ranging from rose-red to soft pink were derived from gold. It is important to remember that a study of the changing colors and use of color is of value in the attempt to learn origin and date of making—for all pottery and enameled wares.

The brilliant colors used in the decoration of porcelain of the K'ang Hsi reign became known as "famille verte" (literally, the green family). In the following period the reign of Yung Cheng, the greens became paler in tone. These colors were gradually replaced by rose-reds—the crimson and pink hues derived from gold, hence the name, "famille rose." The background is often of a soft pink tone called "rouge d'or" (red derived from gold).

During the reign of Yung Cheng (1723–1795), the colors produced at the imperial potteries in Ching-te-chen, copied from originals of the Sung dynasty, included rose-crimson, pyrus pink, aubergine purple, plum, mule's liver mixed with horse's lung (red), dark purple, yellow millet, a bright yellow derived from antimony, sky blue, and other combinations (Dr. Bushell[6]).

Before leaving the subject of chinaware, it seems appropriate to define a much overworked expression, "chinoiserie." The term was coined (probably about 1900) to mean a specimen of Chinese manners, art, decoration, etc. Because of the craze for anything Chinese, (especially during the period 1870 to 1915) it was made to fit the fashion.

JADE

Jade is the common name given to three distinct but closely related minerals: nephrite, jadeite, and chloromelanite. When other minerals are present, the color of nephrite or jadeite may be different shades of green, yellow, brown, red, or black. When no other mineral is present, jade is pure white, described by the Chinese as having the color of mutton fat or congealed lard. If carved thin enough, jade may approach the translucency of fine porcelain.

Color, of itself, is not a reliable factor in determining the value of a piece of jade—either in the rough or in the finished carving. Expertness in this field is hard to come by; it usually requires special equipment to measure hardness, specific gravity, toughness, and the like. There are several different and much less valuable minerals which are often passed off as jade. These imitations fall into three classes: those which bear a natural similarity to jade; those which have been treated or colored to look like jade; those which have none of the virtues of pure jade.

Although the Chinese have always revered this stone above all others, little or no jade seems actually to have been obtained in eastern China. Records indicate that the two nearest sources were Chinese Turkestan (in western Sinkiang province) and Upper Burma. Regardless of its source, Chinese-carved jade has always been of very superior quality of workmanship. Because of its toughness and hardness, jade is a most difficult material to cut or to carve—on the Mohs scale of hardness it ranges from 6 to 7. From ancient times, the Chinese have made use of other minerals having a higher degree of hardness—sapphire, quartz, corundum for their tools. The crystal or stone is mounted in a stylus or bow drill.

Jade is ice-cold to the touch; it emits a musical note when struck; it takes a high, waxy polish—sometimes an oily luster. In the inspection of a piece of jade, a knowledge of these characteristics is not enough—thanks to the prevalence of clever imitations—to warrant an opinion other than "probable."

BRONZES, IVORIES, AND LACQUERS

The student and collector of enameled wares will be more appreciative of their place in Chinese art if at least a cursory knowledge of similar work is acquired. Bronzes, ivories, and lacquers are three categories of distinctive and highly perfected art, uniquely Chinese in character.

There is reliable evidence that various objects of bronze were being made as far back as 2000 B.C. Caldrons, bells, and vases—all of high quality workmanship—were being designed and made for religious and ceremonial use by the end of the Chou dynasty. Even from ancient times, these bronzes carried generous inscriptions and now supply valuable information on the language, customs, and nature of living in that remote period. Various forms of dragons and other mythical monsters, with complex designs in scrolls and "clouds," covered the surface of the vessels.

Unlike the extreme scarcity of records on the history of enamels, bronzes have been written about in a long series of books by Chinese authors, back as far as the sixth century. The text was often accompanied by extremely well-done illustrations. Dr. Bushell has written an exceptionally good account on this subject.[6]

To give an idea of the outstanding ability of the Chinese bronze founder, the records report that, in the fifth century, a bronze statue weighing sixty-five tons was cast. In size and perfection, this would tax any modern foundry. The proportions of the ingredients used in bronzemaking have changed with the centuries. Originally, tin was used in a proportion of one part to five parts of copper; eventually, the tin to copper ratio became as high as one to one. Changes in the composition change the color of the finished bronze; thus the color helps to determine the age of a specific piece. No modern art lover can claim to have even the rudiments of art appreciation so long as he neglects the highly technical, painstaking workmanship inherent in Chinese bronzes.

Ivory carving is mentioned here because, in the technical excellence of the work, it again emphasizes the desire and the unique ability of the Chinese artist to carry out the most intricate and delicate designs. This branch of Chinese art has been criticized on the somewhat debatable premise that the result was more often an exhibition of patient skill than one of aesthetic value. The question might be better appreciated if one were to try to carve, or even to design, the most simple type of drawing on ivory—and compare it with a sample of Chinese work.

In China, ivory carving ranked second to jade carving. As to the source of the ivory used, records dating back to the sixth century B.C. speak of the existence of elephants native to China. With the increase in demand, there came a depletion of the supply of native ivory, making it necessary to import from south Asian countries (India and Burma) and, by the twelfth century after Christ, from Africa. The Chinese also made use of other sources of ivory, such as the walrus, narwhal, mammoth, and rhinoceros; the tusk of the last named is more accurately described as horn.

The Chinese produced a wide range of designs, from chopsticks and fans to intricately pierced and carved spheres-within-spheres and model pavilions a yard square. The most extensive period of carving seems to have been from the thirteenth to the seventeenth century. In contrast to the makers of enameled ware, the ivory carvers were able to design and work in three dimensions—even more freely than in many of the bronzes. Dr.

Bushell[6] has given an excellent account of the subject in every particular.

Lacquer and the lacquer work to be discussed here originated in China and were developed and perfected by that country far beyond the work done in any other part of the world except Japan. According to the records, lacquer was first "discovered" in about the tenth century B.C. The art of working with lacquers advanced through the centuries—in variety of technic, materials inlaid into the lacquer, colors evolved, and the kind of object to which the decoration was applied.

As commonly used, the term "lacquer" covers three distinctly different kinds of material and should not be confused with each other:

1. Chinese and Japanese lacquer was entirely derived from the sap of the lac tree, *Rhus Vernicifera* (varnish-bearing sumac), a tree native to China and Japan.

2. Lac (after refinement, the term "shellac" is used) is the resinous coating exuded by certain types of insects, which live on various kinds of trees in India and neighboring countries. Shellac varies in color, the most valuable being pale orange; when bleached it is known as white shellac.

3. Artificial mixtures, sold under the general title of lacquer, are made from a resin-based varnish, usually applied in a thin coat to wood or metal to protect it from tarnishing.

The process of obtaining the sap of the lac tree and its subsequent treatment and purification is a difficult one. Because of its peculiar properties, this type of lac becomes a natural plastic: highly resistant to water, capable of being engraved or carved, may be colored with a variety of pigments, and can be given a high polish.

Wood, the usual base for the article to be lacquered, is carefully prepared and finished; the successive coats of lacquer (from three to eighteen or more) add the needed strength to the fan, cup, box, or other object to be decorated. The design is often quite complex but always aesthetically pleasing and amazingly precise. A three-dimension effect could be obtained by meticulously carving down through the vari-colored layers, according to the preconceived design of the artist. The art has never been approached in brilliance, design, and workmanship by any other country except Japan. Gold leaf, silver, and mother-of-pearl were often used to enhance the beauty of the final work.

This brief outline of some of the arts of China, other than the work done in enamels, has been included because they all have certain elements in common: Chinese conception, technic, and superior execution. Time would not be wasted in a study of the other arts, such as painting, silk weaving and textile work, sculpture in stone, etc. A knowledge of the history, principles of execution, and the subject matter portrayed—all would help to give a better understanding of the concepts underlying the arts discussed in the previous pages.

CHAPTER VIII

꧞꧁ꪛꫜꪛꫜꪛꫜꪛꫜꪛꫜꪛꫜ꧂꧞

Japanese Enamels: Methods of Creation

*T*HE CHINESE, as has been stated, used the term "Fu-lin ware" in referring to the art of enameling. The word "Fo-lang" was specifically applied to cloisonné enamels. Among the Japanese, the general term "Shippo" was and is used to designate all forms of enameling—champlevé and cloisonné. Literally translated, the word means "seven treasures," because the effect of a finished piece of cloisonné enamel was like that of the seven precious things: gold, silver, emerald, coral, agate, crystal, and pearl.

Although Jiro Harada, a Japanese expert and writer on all branches of his native art, considers the word "Shippo" the most appropriate to use, others have claimed that the proper term should be "Shippo-Yaki." To further confuse the matter, Kaji Ksunekichi (who revived the art of making cloisonné enamels in 1832 or 1839) called it "Oranda-Yaki"—apparently because he thought it resembled the painted Dutch ware being made at that time. This explanation is offered in order to clarify the various terms found in non-Japanese literature.

By contrast with the Chinese process of making cloisonné wares, the Japanese experimented with and perfected highly technical and difficult variations on the Chinese method—in materials used, the use and nonuse of cloisons, and in new and fantastic ways of "rainbowing" colors.

As a preface to Harada's unique and informative account of

the various methods, the following excerpt is so very pertinent that its frankness should be appreciated (exact copy) [13]:

> There are two more or less distinct types of enamel work, one designed for foreign markets, and the other for the home (Japanese) market—at least for the present time. However, in SHIPPO, the distinction between the two types is not so well marked as in other (Japanese) crafts as cloisonné has not yet won an honored place in the Japanese home. It may be added that an incongruous combination of gay and brilliant colors is generally considered the prime factor in "foreign taste," whereas harmonious blending of subdued tones is essential in order to appeal to the more aesthetic sense of the Japanese.

[Note that the above statement was published in 1911.]

Harada's list of the various kinds of enameled ware is as follows:

1. Shippo, the name for all Japanese enamels, champlevé and cloisonné
2. Doro-jippo, opaque enamels
3. Suki-jippo, translucent enamels
4. Yusen-jippo, ordinary work, using cloisons
5. Yusen-do-jippo, a cloisonné enamel on a copper base
6. Gin-jippo, transparent enamel on a silver base
7. Kin-jippo, transparent enamel on a gold base
8. Gin-bari, copper base is first covered with silver "paper" or foil, to show through the enamel
9. Musen-jippo, the temporary cloisons removed after the paste is applied
10. Shotai-jippo, after firing, both cloisons and base are removed
11. Kyoto-jippo, no enamel used; the entire design made of gilt wire
12. Nagare-gusuri, no cloisonné design; entire surface covered with rainbow enamel

METHODS OF CREATION

The base for the cloisonné enameled ware is a piece of copper, silver, or gold hammered out to the desired shape and made smooth. If the base is copper, the cloisons are usually copper, sometimes silver, or brass. If the base is silver, the cloisons are silver. The fusing or melting point of the enamel is in the neighborhood of 1560° Fahrenheit. The formulas for making the various colors of enamel—the relative proportions of glass and oxides, etc.—have been perfected only after long and tedious experimentation and are therefore a closely guarded secret of the artist. The final step is to fit the base and bands to the finished piece—a step not always done in certain ware.

The problem of learning the various methods of attaching the cloisons to the metal base, as used by the Japanese at any time— past or present—has been a difficult one. Those references given in the Bibliography provide only a most cursory description. The most interesting, and apparently the most authentic, account which could be located, is an article of fifteen pages, written by Mrs. (no given name) Hart; it is entitled "Cloisonné and Cloisonné Makers in Japan." The copy in Harvard's Widner Library, KH 929, has the title, "Extracted from Manchester Guardian—Sat. Dec. 12, 1891." The following excerpt is given because it indicates the degree of Mrs. Hart's research, at a time of maximum production of cloisonné ware in Japan:

> The process of making cloisonné enamels is simple, minute and laborious. The design is first sketched on the copper surface to be decorated. Strips of copper about a millimeter in width are then bent with small pincers to correspond to the design and are affixed edgewise to the copper surface by means of a strong glue cement made from the bulb of an orchid, Bletia Hyacinthina. When the cement is dry, the cloisons are soldered to the base. It may interest mechanics to know how the Japanese make their solder. It is 8 parts brass, 7 parts tin, 10 of zinc, melted together. The alloy is then pulverized and 10 parts are mixed with three parts of borax and sufficient water to make a pulpy paste. This paste is

then applied with a stick to the parts to be soldered and then the piece is heated over a moderate coal fire till the solder melts.

The Japanese created a wide range of enamels—transparent, translucent, opaque, and opalescent. Because each color had its own best fusing point, it was necessary to fire the piece accordingly. Each color paste was kept in a separate saucer and applied with either a bamboo stylet, or perhaps an ivory pen. The artist who performed this step had to be thoroughly familiar with the relation between the color of the paste and what it would become after firing.

One step in the enameling process which has been generally overlooked by writers on the subject is that of "counter enameling"—the enamel applied to the underside or inside of the article. The Japanese found this step necessary for two reasons. The first and most important is that when enamel is applied to metal and fired, the metal contracts more than the glass enamel during the cooling. As a result, the metal is likely to warp or the enamel to crack—or "craze"—especially if it is a thin translucent layer. When the back of the metal base is covered with enamel at the time of the first application to the front, both sides will pull evenly during the cooling period and safety of the vessel is assured.

The second reason for the application of a thin layer of enamel to the back side of the base is because the Japanese often used extremely thin and malleable metal—copper or silver; the counter enamel added strength and rigidity to the whole. There are many examples of Japanese enameled ware in which the total thickness—metal plus enamel—is little more than that of a post card.

The counter enamel was usually a thin paste, which was brushed or sprayed onto the base. The color was usually blue or green, left-over material not otherwise needed. With the back side covered with counter enamel and the raw edges finished with a separate metal band—usually of brass, it became difficult to determine the kind of metal used for the base. Although this step

solved a dificult problem, the reason for doing it has been criticized by some writers.

With the increase in demand for enamels—especially outside Japan, large quantities were made for the export trade. The
following excerpt, exactly as written, is taken from a pamphlet is-
sued by the Ando Cloisonne Co., Ltd. of Tokyo, Nagoya, and
Osaka, in 1965:

> Ando Cloisonne Co., Ltd. has been renowned and appraised
> since 1880, when the grandson of Tsunekichi Kaji (Originator of
> the modern cloisonne technique) was appointed as the chief artist
> thereof.
>
> Since the great stride were made in the improvement of tech-
> niques and our company was fortunate to have on its staff, many
> of Japan's famous Shippo artists. Shibataro Kawade was one of the
> excellent staff members who was the chief factor in discovering the
> new techniques of cloisonne in the middle of the Meiji era, when
> the Tokyo store was opened on Ginza.

Gin-bari was one of the favorites made for the foreign trade.
The first step in this type of work was to apply a thin coat of
enamel to the copper base; to the fired foundation is then added a
layer of silver "paper" or foil, carefully smoothed into place. The
foil may then be pebbled or tinted to suit the design before the
final coat of transparent enamel is added. The silver foil may be
confined to the cloison design or cover the entire piece. If foil is
not used outside the design, that part of the article is covered with
an opaque enamel.

In the cloisonné ware called Musen-jippo, an entirely different effect is obtained. The design is drawn on the article in the
usual fashion, temporary cloisons placed, and the varicolored
pastes applied. After the work has dried, the cloisons are carefully
removed before the piece is fired. In some cases, the cloisons are
relaid in a different design, another layer of paste is applied, and
the firing is repeated. Transparent enamels are used in this kind of
work.

Shotai-jippo is probably the most difficult variation in enamel
work. In this process, the cloisons and paste are placed in the usual

way; after firing, the metal—base and cloisons—is removed by chemical means, leaving only a stained glass effect. The French term Plique-à-jour was applied to the rare examples of this kind of work done in Europe.

Another variation in Japanese enameling is undoubtedly a result of their long experience and expertness in metal working and metal inlays for ornamental purposes. In one method, an inset of a contrasting kind of metal, perhaps gold or bronze, is made—with the entire remaining surface of the article covered with a transparent enamel of a contrasting color.

In addition to the twelve principal kinds of enamel work previously listed, there are others in which a special effect is obtained: Moriagé, in which the surface is slightly raised in relief by means of adding an extra amount of enamel; Uchidashi, in which the metal base is hammered up into a relief effect as required by the design; Akasuké, in which the base is usually given a carved design and covered with transparent enamel, without cloisons; Usuji, when the single-color enamel base is of a light color rather than dark; Kodai-moyo, in which the design is patterned after the old Chinese pondweed, a vine-like scroll, the cloisons usually being quite heavy in this type of work; Nagare-gusuri, in which the rainbow colored enamel runs down in the manner of a porcelain glaze.

Another (unnamed) example of Japanese work, similar to Kyoto-jippo, builds a design of extra-large cloisons, filled in with opaque enamels and polished down to the top of the cloison. In this type of work, the remainder of the surface is bare metal, and the over-all effect similar to filigree work.

Another feature, distinctive of Japanese enamel work, is the type of cloison used. Combinations of twisted-ribbon spirals and circles are used in various designs, comparatively heavy in contrast to the very fine cloisons making up the remainder of the design. The twisted-ribbon cloison gives the appearance of a tiny twisted rope. There is some evidence that this type of work may have originated in Korean enamel work, but cannot be verified.

Before leaving this discussion of the various kinds of Japanese

Copper cup and saucer, Japanese.

Copper teapot, Japanese, two and one-half inches high and six inches in diameter. Extremely complex design of ho-ho birds and multicolored butterflies covering top, bottom and handle.

Vase, Japanese, six inches high. Silver cloisons on copper. Two birds
with wisteria and other flowers on dark blue ground.

enamel work, as described by Harada, the following notes are of interest, as taken from the Frank Brinkley treatise, *Japan and China*, Vol. VII. He states that cloisonné enamels on metals, known in Japanese as *kazari-jippo*, means "ornamental enamel." He continues (exactly as written):

> Grinding and polishing is often dispensed with, especially when translucent pastes are employed. Enamel decoration of the latter class is called *nagashi-jippō* poured enamel.

All Japanese words in Brinkley's book are in italics. Note the bar over the o in jippo; the use of this bar, both for shippo and jippo, is not consistently done in the various references cited. Note also that the two Japanese names employed by Brinkley differ from those included in the Harada articles.[13]

As the Japanese artisan became more experienced in the art of enameling, he found that it was not necessary to use cloisons in order to hold the enamel in place without chipping off. In a large proportion of the work produced, the design occupied only a minor portion of the space—the major part being entirely devoid of cloisons, covered with the uninterrupted enamel. This fact is of special importance because of the erroneous statement sometimes made that the Chinese filled the background with scrolls, clouds, and the like, in order to "support" the enamel. So far as can be learned, there is nothing in the Chinese records to warrant this assumption. It is likely that use was made of the powdered ground—by both the Chinese and the Japanese artist—if and when that was the effect desired.

HISTORY

Based on available records, Japan was the first country to produce cloisonné enamels on any base other than metal. The ancient Assyrians and Egyptians produced marvellous glazes and enamels on brick and pottery, but the process was entirely different and no cloisons were used. On this subject there is the usual lack of reliable information, native or foreign.

In his book *Oriental Ceramic Art*, published in 1899, S. W.
Bushell states that the first cloisonné on porcelain was made about
1870. James L. Bowes,[4] in connection with his criticism that
"modern enamels" (meaning those made during the period 1850 to
1884) "merit only passing notice," has this to say:

> The earlier enamels on porcelain were made clearly in imita-
> tion of the ancient works upon copper, the dark greens having
> been closely copied; but the pastes used were very soft, the nature
> of the foundation requiring that they should be vitrified at a low
> temperature, and the surfaces show none of the brilliant polish
> which is found on the genuine ware.
>
> This branch of manufacture has largely developed during the
> past ten years, and immense quantities of porcelain partially, or
> entirely, covered with cloisonné decoration have been sent to Eu-
> rope and America.

To comment on the above statements, it is entirely a matter
of opinion whether a hard, polished surface is more desirable than
a softer, eggshell surface. Porcelain or bisque, each has merit.
Whether intense or pale, the design and the colors can be equally
harmonious and beautiful. Enamels on porcelain need not be vitri-
fied at a low temperature; most glass enamels fuse at a temperature
below 1600° F. while porcelain or semiporcelain does not fuse
below 2300° to 2600°. The apparent explanation is that Bowes
(whose book was published in 1884) had not seen any of the ware
produced by such artists as Namakawa of Kyoto. In this ware, the
surface is as hard and the colors as intense as any "found on the
genuine ware," apparently referring to polychrome-painted porcelain.

Examples of cloisonné on porcelain, or other ceramic ware,
are comparatively rare in the United States, to the extent that few
antique dealers recognize them as such. When porcelain was used
as a base, the cloisons were cemented to the previously fired body,
a procedure made necessary because porcelain fuses at a temperature several hundred degrees higher than brass, copper, or silver.
The vitreous enamels, used by such artists as Namakawa of Kyoto,
covered the entire article (vase, etc.) although the design occupied

only a small part of the space. The result, in color and delicacy of workmanship, compared favorably with painted porcelain. A softer, eggshell finish was obtained when the base was a soft-paste porcelain.

Namakawa Yasuyuki of Kyoto is known to have produced cloisonné on porcelain late in the nineteenth century. An example of his work, in the possession of the writer, is a combination of perfect design, workmanship, and color.

CHAPTER IX

Japanese Enamels: Design and Symbolism

ONE of the most important of the requisites for a proper appreciation of Japanese enamels is a working knowledge of the symbolism inherent in this branch of art. It is difficult to understand how an intelligent appraisal of the aesthetic values can be made otherwise.

Any study of design and symbolism in Japan—regardless of the kind of art involved—must take into account the relation, physically and historically, of three countries: China, Korea, and Japan. Confusion exists because ideals in art were similar in the three countries and there is far from sufficient knowledge as to how this came about. The usual theory is that art ideals, methods of working, and the like traveled from China to Korea and thence to Japan.

In trying to solve the question of country of origin, it is well to remember that the Japanese are known to have copied, more or less closely, Chinese enamel designs. At the same time, there is a wide divergence of opinion on the subject. A careful study of the characteristics of authenticated pieces is probably the best way by which to learn to distinguish the origin of those in question.

In Japanese cloisonné enamels, design follows the widest possible range, from extremely fine geometrical patterns, through realistic figures of men and animals, to sketchy landscapes—or no design at all. This slowly changing trend followed, or was followed by, the change in use: first, in the temples and palaces; second, in the homes of those Japanese who appreciated this type of art; third, to supply the overwhelmingly eager foreign trade. Mainly because early Japanese enamels were designed for and were to be kept in the most revered places in their country, they were to be accepted as examples of virtu—priceless because of exquisitely precise workmanship rather than for decorative value. Only when this premise is accepted will the merits of the early ware be properly appreciated.

Early Japanese enameled ware include temple lamps, flower vases, covered jars (which may have been used to hold the powdered tea used in religious ceremonies), and various kinds of dishes—trays or platters, square, round, and oval. There were also tables of various sizes and shapes for various uses—and tea or water pots. Some of these pieces had unbound edges or protecting rim, even though the metal of the body was very thin. Others had bound edges—rims of a gilded metal to protect and strengthen the thin body. Because of the extreme rarity of this early ware, except in museums or some private collections, about the only way to study the designs is by means of pictures.

A pattern common to much of the Japanese enamels is the combination of one or more medallions or "pictures" on an article, surrounded by a background or "grounds" of delicate, winding scrolls and of small, serrated half-leaves of China grass ("Kara Kusa"). Sometimes in addition to the scrolls were many fan-shaped medallions made up of an endless variety of minute diapers. The principal medallion was occupied by such creatures of the mythological world as the dragon, phoenix, or "kirin" (a lion). But rarely, in the early work, were found the graceful characteristics of their Chinese originals. In later work, the figures become more charming, the colors more lively.

Japanese design is an ever-changing variety of symbolic things—chimerical fauna and fanciful flora—and later, in a generous use of butterflies and birds. Other characters and symbols indicate longevity, happiness, etc. A brief description of some of the more important and prevalent mythological creatures and more realistic figures should help to explain the symbolism involved.

THE DRAGON

This fantastic creature is related to the Chinese dragon in form and characteristics, except that the Japanese version varies about as often as the artist who conceived it. Whereas the Chinese dragon almost always has five claws (sometimes four) for each of his four legs, the Japanese dragon almost always has three claws (rarely four). In design, a Japanese dragon has more of the attributes of a sea horse or a wiggly reptile, with the head more often in profile than that of his Chinese cousin. Contrary to the usual conception of a European dragon, neither the Chinese nor Japanese dragon had wings and they did not always have an evil reputation. While essentially a snaky sort of beast, it always had four legs, a supernaturally sharp pair of eyes and, in its way, it was a highly feared dragon.

Because so little has been written on the subject of the Japanese dragon, the following excerpt from the Japanese writer, Bakin, might help the average reader to recognize one:

> The dragon is a creature of a very superior order of being. It has a deer's horns, a horse's head, eyes like those of a devil, a neck like that of a snake, a belly like that of a red worm, scales like those of a fish, claws like a hawk's, paws like a tiger's, and ears like those of a cow. . . .

It should be added that the dragon has a pair of wicked jaws with wolf-like fangs, also streamers of fire spouting from the body. In spite of its wrathy look, it is often a friendly dragon. The dragon was capable of changing size at will, even to the point of becoming invisible; it was decidedly unsociable, preferring to live alone. In the winter it lived dormant, in the spring it ascended to the heavens, in the summer it sported around in the clouds, and in the autumn it again descended to the water, usually a river. The mikado or emperor took on himself the attributes of the dragon—even his attire was called the "dragon robes."

THE HO-HO BIRD

For lack of an English translation for this mythical bird, it is necessary to use the Japanese term, as described by Bowes.[4] Although the symbolism is different, it is obviously related to the Chinese Phoenix. It has been described as an "imaginary but beautiful Bird of Paradise." Even so, some credit should be given the Japanese imagination because the nearest habitat of the Bird of Paradise is New Guinea, three thousand miles from Canton.

The ho-ho is not as fierce looking as the phoenix, but is always depicted, especially in Japanese enamels, as the most graceful and colorful product of the Japanese imagination. The head of a ho-ho resembles that of a peacock; its tail feathers more nearly resemble those of a bird of paradise, except there are invariably three graceful plumes. The coloration of the entire bird is varied to harmonize with the rest of the design. The ho-ho is almost always shown in flight, a feature which adds to the rhythm of the design. A favorite combination in Japanese cloisonné work is a ho-ho, sometimes framed in a medallion, surrounded by butterfiles and chrysanthemums. The bird apparently symbolizes the majesty and culture of the emperor.

THE CHRYSANTHEMUM OR KIKU CREST

Probably the most common symbol used in Japanese cloisonné work is the chrysanthemum. It is usually drawn as a full flower, in the form of a wheel, from realistic to idealistic and in various colors to harmonize with the general design. It may be shown as a single "wheel" of petals, ranging in number from twelve to eighteen, or as a double-petal wheel in which the number may run as high as thirty-one. It has been the national flower of Japan for centuries, and as such is included in the design of the Imperial crest, as a badge of the emperor and of certain nobles. As an emblem of authority, only the emperor could have the flower shown with sixteen petals; later, the rule seems to have been broadened to include members of the imperial family.

One reason for the popularity of the chrysanthemum is that it is known as the Flower of Happiness. It should be kept in mind that the presence of a kiku crest in a cloisonné design does not, of itself, indicate the quality of the specimen. Only when the over-all excellence of design, workmanship, and color is notable on all three counts does the symbolism give added merit.

THE KIRI CREST

The kiri crest or symbol is an exclusively Japanese design and is often used in combination with the kiku badge; it also was reserved for the emperor and his family.

The design consists of the leaves and flowers of the paulownia tree. There is confusion as to how the paulownia tree—also known as the Emperor or Empress Tree—got its name. Whether it was named after a Russian dancer or a princess of Holland does not alter the fact that the tree is a native of Japan and has been symbolic of the royal family for centuries. It was brought to the United States in the nineteenth century and may be found in the eastern section, in such cities as Washington, Baltimore, and Philadelphia. It is an extremely fast growing tree.

The leaves of the paulownia are heart-shaped, somewhat similar to the catalpa. The leaf, as depicted in Japanese enamels, may be simple or with three lobes. The flowers grow in bunches or panicles, similar to those on a buckeye tree; they are similar in shape to a foxglove or catalpa and are a pretty purplish-violet. The usual cloisonné design consists of a group of three leaves; three stems of flowers spring from the leaves, sometimes in a close cluster of from three to seven flowers per stem; sometimes from ten to thirty flowers, spaced along the gracefully curving stem. The design may also include a few single-cloison tendrils. Whether there is a significance to the number of buds per stem cannot be determined. Although the kiri crest was freely used as a part of the decoration in enamel work, it was not used on painted porcelains; no explanation has been found for this rule.

FLOWERS

The decoration of Japanese enamels is quite as diverse as that previously described for Chinese ware, but the symbolism does not appear to be pronounced. The use of flowers, leaves, and vines seems to be primarily to create an intricate and beautiful design. Of the flowers used in the enamels, the prunus and peony are the most common.

The term "prunus" covers members of the peach, plum, prune, and cherry family. In design, the blossom is usually shown with five petals, fully open; the petal is shown in oval form, sometimes heart-shaped similar to a dogwood blossom, sometimes with a pointed tip. For many centuries, the Japanese have cherished their plum and cherry trees; their flowers have long been favorites in their art and poetry.

The peony blossom, always shown fully open and in realistic style, is usually the Tree Peony—the flowers grow on half-woody stems. It is the same as the Chinese Peony Moutan. In Japanese designs, it takes the place of the Chinese Lotus blossom—symbolic of Buddhism. The peony is almost always shown in various shades of red and in a fanciful variety of flowing designs.

OTHER EMBLEMS

The butterfly is one of the most popular and graceful figures to be found in Japanese enamels. It appears, always flying, in designs, colors, and sizes—from minute to one occupying a whole medalion—as a beautiful example of the Oriental imagination. Its significance lies apparently in its carefree flight among the other parts of the design.

KARA-KUSA, also known as China grass or pondweed, is an ornamental vine meandering over the surface of the design, sometimes as a double-cloison stem, sometimes in single-cloison tendrils—usually in contrasting colors.

TSURU OR CRANE, either flying or standing—but always very gracefully drawn—is a Japanese emblem of longevity. In color it is usually white or gray. The design may include only two or three—or as many as twenty or more.

OTHER FIGURES FOUND IN ENAMELS include the eagle—or a bird similiar to it—and many other birds, usually flying in the composition of Japanese ware. Trees, such as bamboo, willow, and fir, each has a significant place in the symbolism. Other flowers, not previously named, such as the wistaria, iris, and poppy may be found in enameled ware as beautifully done as that to be found in painted porcelain. Fowl—ducks and chickens—are a favorite subject appearing in the more rare types of work. A final example of the Japanese imagination is the "Kirin"—a sort of lionish chimera, rarely seen in enamels. It is supposed to be the offspring of a dragon and a cow.

CHAPTER X

Color in Japanese Enamels

$\mathcal{T}$*HE STUDY* of color in Japanese enamel ware is important not only for its contribution to the aesthetic value of a particular specimen, but also because it can be a vital factor in the determination of age. Some of the early ware—being more desirable for its age—may not be as artistic, by Western standards, as later work.

As is the case with Chinese enamel work, there are few reliable records to describe the extremely difficult problems faced by the early Japanese artisan in his quest for satisfactory colors. As Harada [13] points out, it is a national trait to strive for fine workmanship—the most intricate designs and technique—rather than to emphasize artistic decoration.

Early enamels made use of such varied colors as pink, yellow, red, blue, white, green, and purple. The base color or background was usually a dark green, sometimes blue or white. Later, near the end of the nineteenth century, a pale blue took the place of the dark green. In listing the various colors, it is emphasized that it is difficult to describe the specific tone or hue of each one. In general, the color is subdued in tone, that is, not as bright or vivid as in later work, or as those colors so much used in Chinese enamels. The use of a cloudy blue or a somber green may have been partly due, in the early work, to inexperience.

The small cloisonné inserts in Japanese sword guards were

79

done in opaque or translucent enamels; this type of work is generally attributed to the middle and later part of the eighteenth century. In the early work done after the "rediscovery" of enamel making, some time after 1839, only opaque enamels were used, at least those enamels known to the Western world. Probably beginning about 1870, translucent or transparent enamels were increasingly employed—with a brighter and more varied spectrum of colors, including mottled and opalescent effects.

Whether the increase in the use of more vivid colors is due to a change of ideals in Japan or a sharp increase in foreign demand for enamels is a moot point. Beautiful shades of red, brilliant blues, fresh greens, gemlike tones of lilac, pink, and yellow became common. The pinks and reds were probably derived from gold. As in the other colors, the subtle shades of gray owe their essence to the precise proportion of potash used in the flux. Harada states that gray was discovered ". . . by the mere smell of wood by a Japanese artisan." [13] Study and untiring experimentation by trial and error were inherent characteristics far beyond the comprehension of the average artist.

One feature of translucent enamels, first discovered and used by the Japanese artist, is usually described as "sparkle." This effect, often found throughout the background, is created by one of two similar methods. Harada describes the first method from which the following excerpt is taken [13]: "[Then] the case of the craftsman who stumbled on the secret of *chakin* (tea gold) while experimenting with copper, some shavings of which fell into the molten enamel and gave an exquisite golden lustre." Being imbedded in the translucent or transparent enamel, the tiny copper shavings retain their golden sparkle, an effect similar to but superior to that obtained by the use of "goldstone."

Goldstone is a glass imitation of yellow or red aventurine; it contains small crystals of metallic copper, buried in clear glass. Real aventurine is quartz inclosing tiny scales of mica or hematite. One variety, known as "Sunstone," is found in the U.S., Norway, and near Lake Baikal in northern Mongolia. The effect obtained by the Japanese artisan is entirely different than either aventurine or goldstone would give, at least as indicated by available evidence.

In the second method used by the Japanese enameler to obtain a sparkling effect, tiny bits of silver foil are buried in the translucent or transparent enamel—in the same way that copper shavings are. The foil takes on the color of the enamel used: silver, gold, green, purple, or mottled. A close examination is required to distinguish between the copper-shaving and the silver-foil method.

CHAPTER XI

❄︎⸜⸝⸜⸝⸜⸝⸜⸝⸜⸝⸜⸝❄︎

Distinctions Between Chinese and Japanese Enamels

*I*N THE FIELD of enameled ware, Chinese or Japanese, the twin questions of origin and age present a frustrating problem, as evidenced by the records—and the lack of them. Just as the Chinese had learned the art of enameling, probably from Byzantine sources, but had developed methods and designs peculiarly their own, so did the Japanese eventually create enameled work which was entirely distinctive. (It should be kept in mind, however, that being able to distinguish between the work of one country and that of another is not as important as being able to recognize the characteristics of a superior piece of enamel compared with one of mediocre merit.)

The following list of distinguishing characteristics applies primarily to the grade of enamels in the average collection, outside of a museum. Inasmuch as many of the exhibits in even the best of museums lack specific identification, it should be understood that the following observations must serve until a better guide is devised:

1. The majority of enameled ware, either in a collection or for sale, is Japanese.

2. Champlevé enamel on bronze is Chinese. Estimate of age cannot depend on the assumption that the Chinese had not made champlevé before the eighteenth century as sometimes claimed. It must be estimated by a study of design, workmanship, degree of pitting, etc. Color is also very important.

3. Cloisonné on bronze is rarely Japanese. The Chinese added handles, finials, and fittings—either made as a part of the body or added separately. Exposed bronze was gilded.

4. The cloisons used in early Chinese work were bronze and coarse; they became smaller and thinner with later work, of copper or brass, depending on the nature of the design. Even from the beginning, Japanese cloisons were exceedingly fine, of copper or silver. Cloisons were not used at all in some work.

5. In Chinese cloisonné work, the cell was always filled to the level of the cloison and the enamel polished. In Japanese work, there are examples in which the cell was only partially filled and the enamel left with a "fire polish."

6. Opaque enamels were used almost entirely by the Chinese, for all work except for a base of gold or silver. Opaque enamels were used by the Japanese in early work but in later work they were used in conjunction with translucent and semi-translucent enamels, often on the same piece. In other work, the Japanese used transparent or translucent entirely on some of their ware, according to the effect desired.

7. The Chinese always used heavier and thicker base material in their cloisonné work; the Japanese made the body of the ware of very thin copper. As one dealer said, "If it's dented, it's Japanese." While the rule is hardly polite, it does describe the result of misuse.

8. Painted enamels on copper with entirely opaque enamel or with the design in a medallion surrounded by a cloisonné background are Chinese.

9. Enameled ware—cloisonné, painted, etc.—has been made by various European countries since the tenth century. It is not always possible to determine the source from the design or workmanship.

10. A vessel with a cloisonné design occupying only a small part of the area, the remainder in plain enamel without cloisons, is always Japanese.

11. Enameled ware, with a design but without cloisons, is Japanese; the cloisons have been removed before firing.

12. Cloisonné with transparent enamel on silver foil is Japanese.

13. Cloisonné enamels on porcelain or semi-porcelain are of Japanese make; the enamel is always opaque.

14. "Sparkle" is always Japanese; it was never used in Chinese work.

15. The coarse square scroll, known as the Greek key or fret pattern, is Chinese; it was copied from ancient bronzes.

16. Geometric designs and arabesques (in the Arabian fashion) are Chinese. Do not confuse with the Japanese diaper work.

17. Ornamental borders in extremely fine fretwork are Japanese. In Chinese work, the border design is larger in comparison to the total area than in Japanese ware, but this feature requires careful study as a part of the total design.

18. Complex diaper patterns are Japanese, especially in early ware; examples of Chinese work are exceedingly rare.

19. The Ogre is always Chinese, whether as a part of the design or cast into the bronze handles or the finial.

20. The Lion, or "Devil Dog," is Chinese—usually as a casting on the top of an incense burner or covered jar.

21. The Dragon is a favorite in both Chinese and Japanese enameled ware. The Chinese dragon has five claws and stares straight out at the world; the Japanese dragon has three claws; his head is usually shown side-face.

22. The Elephant, either standing or lying down, is Chinese.

23. The Bat is Chinese—usually shown in red, in pairs.

24. The Endless Knot or Entrails, "Chang," is Chinese and denotes longevity.

25. The Pearl or Flaming Jewel is Chinese; it is usually shown near the mouth of a dragon.

26. The Phoenix is rarely seen in Chinese cloisonné enamels and is depicted as an eagle-like bird. Its Japanese relative, the Ho-

Bronze vase, Chinese, nine inches high. Five-clawed dragon with flaming pearl (not visible in photograph) and double-cloison clouds on blue ground.

ho or Bird of Paradise, more nearly resembles a peacock and is very common in their enamels.

27. The Swastika is Chinese.

28. Waves and double-cloison Clouds are Chinese.

29. Butterflies are sometimes used in Chinese enamels, painted or in cloisonné, as part of a picture design. Butterflies are very common in Japanese design, either alone in a medallion or as part of the background.

30. The Peach—shown as fruit, flower, and leaves—is Chinese. When used on Japanese enamels, it is shown in schematic rather than in naturalistic form.

31. The Lotus is predominately Chinese, symbolic of Buddhism. The Japanese Tree Peony is drawn similar to the Lotus and to the Chinese Peony. It is often necessary to decide in terms of other factors in a specific piece.

32. The Chrysanthemum is one of the most important of the Japanese motifs used in cloisonné enamels, shown in schematic form as the Kiku crest. When shown in Chinese enamels, it is in naturalistic form.

33. The Kiri crest—the leaves and flowers of the paulownia tree—is always Japanese.

34. The Carnation is Japanese.

35. Leaf scrolls are shown in more realistic or naturalistic form in Chinese work than in Japanese. Pondweed meanders are a typical Japanese design having little resemblance to any of the Chinese work.

36. The color yellow is reserved for royalty in Chinese decoration and is of a butter-cup tone. Japanese yellow is more of a cream or greenish-yellow shade.

37. Green is a distinctive background color in a great proportion of Japanese enameled ware, in contrast to Chinese work which employed green only rarely and then as a part of the design as in naturalistic leaves, etc. While much of the Japanese green was in dark, almost black, shades, the Chinese developed such live tints as cucumber, apple, onion, emerald, and snake-skin green. Turquoise-blue (pale blue) was a favorite background color in Chinese enamels.

CHAPTER XII

❦❦❦❦❦❦❦❦

Care and Cleaning of Enamels

IN SPITE of its importance, available literature says nothing regarding the care and cleaning of enameled ware—champlevé, cloisonné, or painted. Treated with reasonable care, a piece a century old may have all the freshness and brilliance of one only a fraction of its age. One often finds, however, a specimen on the shelf of an antique shop, damaged enough to suggest that sometime in the past it has been used as a nut cracker. It cannot be satisfactorily mended. If the damage has exposed cloisons, a protective coating of a brushing enamel of the proper color may be applied. Even candle wax, dripped on and scraped down to a smooth surface, will hide a blemish quite well.

Even in the better shops handling enameled ware, many of the pieces are so befogged with a coating of tarnish and dirt as to reduced their aesthetic appeal to a minimum. So that it will not be considered an oversight, these remarks are not directed to those who wish to retain a so-called air of antiquity; it might well be that the intrinsic beauty of the enamel is not appreciated.

Under certain circumstances, such as long exposure to grime and moisture, bronze and brass take on a metallic film called patina. This patina is usually green, although it can be various shades of tan or brown; chemically, it protects the surface from further oxidation. The patina on Chinese bronzes, especially on gilded metal, should be left undisturbed. No cleaning agent other than mild soap and warm water should be used. Do not attempt to re-gild the metal.

In order to keep enameled ware, especially the cloisonné type, looking its best and to know the best way to clean it when it becomes dirty, it is unwise to ignore the fact that two entirely different materials are involved—metal and glass. The most appropriate solution for one is rarely the best cleaning agent for the other. In any case, the agent used should not be quite as extreme as that applied by an assistant curator of a large museum; he uses a "secret mixture," consisting mainly of a type of polishing wax. Enamels do not need to be "preserved."

In making a piece of enameled ware, the final step involves first the grinding down of the enamel to the top of the metal divider or cloison, and second, polishing the glass surface to remove every trace of a scratch. The more carefully this work is done, the more nearly perfect will be the result. The grinding agent may be as many as nine whetstones (corundum or sandstone), each of an increasing degree of fineness. Polishing powders include: powdered pumice, crocus, tripoli, magnolia charcoal, and rouge—used with water, also wood ash and rape oil. Over the centuries, many different agents and combinations have been used.

Before any cleaning work is done, a close examination with a strong magnifying glass should be made to determine if the cloisons have become corroded rather than tarnished. If and when this is the case, the results to be obtained through scouring are hardly worth the effort required. Glass enamels are of varying degrees of hardness according to color; a heavy hand is the worst tool to use wherever they are present; patience gives much better results.

The following list of readily available cleaning-polishing agents is arranged in an approximately increasing order of abrasiveness. Transparent or translucent enamels require much more care than the dull-finish opaque types; the last five items should be used only for opaque enameled ware:

1. Glass-cleaning spray
2. Mild liquid soap in warm water

3. Ammonia of the "sudsy" type
4. Lacquer thinner; use only to remove a lacquer coating
5. Silver polish; useful only if the cloisons are silver
6. Brass polish, liquid
7. Powdered pumice (dental type) in clear or ammonia water
8. Powdered pumice with liquid metal ("brass") polish
9. Copper-cleaning or scouring powder, with warm water
10. Corundum or sand paper, No. 6 or finer.

No matter how highly polished the surface of the enamel may look, examination with a magnifying glass may reveal many minute pin-holes in the enamel. It is therefore necessary that any cleaner-polisher, especially those in powder form, must be completely washed off in warm water after use. Apply the cleaner with a soft cloth or sponge. A toothbrush may be used for the more inaccessible parts of a bronze handle or ornament. The cloth used to polish the metal rim or base should not be used for the cloisonné portions of the vessel; light-colored enamels can become stained and are difficult to restore to their original tones. After the article has been carefully rinsed in running warm water, it should be given a dry polish with a soft cloth.

When the value of a specimen warrants it, as much as eight hours of gentle rubbing may be required to regain the original beauty of the enamel and the cloisons. As a fitting finis to this chapter and to a book of this kind, please bear in mind: There is no likelihood we shall ever have any more cloisonné enamels made like those of the past. Take good care of what you have.

Appendices

CHINESE DYNASTIES AND DATES
GLOSSARY
CHINESE PRONUNCIATION
CHINESE-ENGLISH LIST OF SYMBOLS
JAPANESE-ENGLISH LIST OF SYMBOLS
MELTING POINTS OF METALS AND OTHER
MATERIALS

CHINESE DYNASTIES AND DATES

Based on records going back 4,000 years, much of the art of China can be ascribed to a specific dynasty—often to a particular reign in that dynasty. The Chinese had two methods of indicating a date, either of which could eventually be translated into the western calendar.

The first was to date according to the reign of an emperor or king. This was called "nien-hao" and started at the beginning of the first new year after his accession to the throne. The second method computed dates in sixty-year cycles. In some cases, both the reign title and the cyclical character were combined in the "date mark," especially as shown on the bottom of porcelain ware.

A group of rulers or emperors of the same line or family became a dynasty. Because of lack of records covering a period, or the absence of any mark on an article being examined (as enamels), it is often difficult to assign it even to a specific dynasty. The following table lists the various periods of Chinese history; in earlier years the dates may be approximate.

Dynasty		Dates	Years
Hsia (18 rulers)		2205–1767 B.C.	438
Shang and Yin (28 rulers)		1766–1122 B.C.	644
Shang	1766–1401		
Yin	1401–1122		
Chou		1122–255 B.C.	867
Early (6 rulers)	1122–947		
Middle (7 rulers)	947–770		
Late (22 rulers)	770–255		
Ch'in		255–246 B.C.	9
Cheng		246–206 B.C.	40
Han		206 B.C. to A.D. 220	426

Dynasty	Dates	Years
The Six Dynasties	220–589	369
Sui	589–618	29
T'ang	618–906	288
The Five Dynasties	906–960	54
Sung, Northern	960–1127	167
Southern	1127–1280	153
Yüan (Mongolian rulers)	1280–1368	88
Ming, Chinese (17 emperors)	1368–1643	275

Hung Wu	1368–1398		
Chien Wen	1399–1402		
Yung Lo	1403–1424		
Hung Hsi	1425		
Hsuan Te	1426–1435		
Cheng T'ung	1436–1449		
Ching T'ai	1450–1457		
T'ien Shun	1457–1464		
Ch'eng Hua	1465–1487		
Hung Chih	1488–1505		
Cheng Te	1506–1521		
Chia Ching	1522–1566		
Lung Ch'ing	1567–1572		
Wan Li	1573–1619		
T'ai Ch'ang	1620		
T'ien Ch'i	1621–1627		
Ch'ung Cheng	1628–1643		
Ch'ing, Manchu (10 emperors)		1644–1912	268
Shun Chih	1644–1661		
K'ang Hsi	1662–1722		
Yung Cheng	1723–1735		
Ch'ien Lung	1736–1795		
Chai Ch'ing	1796–1820		
Tao Kuang	1821–1850		
Hsien Feng	1851–1861		
T'ung Chih	1862–1873		
Kuang Hsu	1874–1908		
Hsuan T'ung	1909–1912		
Chinese Republic		1912–1949	37
People's Republic of China (Communist)		1949–	

GLOSSARY

archaic–ancient, relating to a more primitive time

aubergine–egg plant or egg plant color; deep purple

aventurine–a variety of translucent quartz, spangled with scales of mica or other minerals. Also, a kind of man-made glass containing copper-like crystals. See goldstone and sunstone.

basse taille–translucent enamel over carved metal

blance de chine–velvety white porcelain

bleu fouetté–powder blue

biscuit–ceramic pottery or porcelain, after first firing

Byzantium–Greek city, on the shores of the Bosporus; site of Constantinople (Istanbul); noted for its fine arts, mainly 300–1400 A.D.

celadon–green in color, or porcelain with green coloring

champlevé–enamel inlaid in chiseled or cut-out ground

chimera–imaginary monster

china–porcelain ware, first made in China

chinoiserie–European (18th century) style of ornamentation using Chinese motifs; an example of such style

clair de lune–pale gray-blue

cloison–metal wire or ribbon which acts as a partition in cloisonné enameling

cloisonné–enamel decoration inlaid between cloisons

cloud–cloison formed into a "cloud" as background in the design; irregular bean-shaped cloisons, similar to cumulus clouds.

date mark–mark indicating date of making; in China, as many as six characters

devil-dog–name sometimes given the Chinese lion or lion-dog (a Buddhist symbol)

diaper–pattern using a repetition of one or more units of design— usually Japanese

famille noire–decoration in black, usually on porcelain

famille rose–decoration in rose—the "rose family"

famille verte–decoration usually in tones of green

fire–to bake, as for pottery or enamel

flux–glass in a molten state, or fusible glass

foliated–leaf shaped

frit–glass in a molten state, or partly fused materials for making glass

gild–to overlay with a thin layer of gold, usually by mechanical means

glaze–vitreous coating for ceramic ware, transparent

glitter–sparkle effect in Japanese enamels, similar to goldstone; like a mass of minute copper triangles buried in the translucent enamel

goldstone–the natural stone is aventurine; the artificial material is glass, cooled in a way to produce partial crystalization

go-down–a warehouse (eastern Asia)

grès–clay mixed with silica, to produce a safe firing temperature without breakage

grisaille–design in which white top enamel is carved to a black base, in cameo style

ground–surface of article, foundation, background

hieratic–consecrated to sacred or religious uses

incise–to cut into the surface; to carve or engrave

jade–a compact stone or mineral, various colors and varicolored— also jadeite or nephrite

kaolin–a pure white clay, used with petuntze to make porcelain

lion–not a native of China, but used as a Buddhist symbol; a defender of the law

lion-dog–fu-lion or "shih"; China's interpretation of a lion, symbolic in form and meaning

lunette–medallion, a crescent shape

medallion–* a medal or design, on porcelain or enamel work

mille fiori–a glass mosaic; ornamental glass, made by fusing together disks of different colors

muffle kiln–a type of oven to protect the contents from the furnace flame

nephrite–a kind of jade, less valuable than jadeite

niello–a black alloy of sulphur combined with lead, copper, and silver.

ogre–a hideous mythical monster; only the head is shown in Chinese work—bronze or enamel

* a panel picture or design with a border or a background in contrast to the surrounding pattern.

patina–a film in various shades of green, formed on copper or bronze by long exposure to a moist atmosphere or by use of acid

petuntze–"China stone," a decomposed stone, used with kaolin to make porcelain

plique-à-jour–cloisonné work from which the base is removed; produces a stained-glass effect

porcelain–a type of chinaware, made with kaolin and petuntze; fine, hard, white, translucent, and resonant

pottery–earthenware, usually made with clay—with or without a glaze

powdered base–a background design on cloisonné work, of dots, circles, spirals, and clouds

prunus–a genus of trees: the plum, cherry and peach; the five-petal blossoms are a common form of decoration in Chinese and Japanese design

pumice–a kind of hardened volcanic glass froth, usually white or gray; in powder form it is used for polishing—an abrasive

rape or rapeseed–a nondrying oil, used as a lubricant with powdered pumice

repoussé–design on thin metal, hammered into relief by working on back side

reticulated–resembling a network; like the threads of a net

rouge–a fine red powder used to polish glass, gems, or metal; jeweler's rouge

roundel–a round form, figure, or circle

sang de boeuf–color of ox-blood, beef red, derived from copper; found in ancient Chinese porcelain

scroll–spiral or coiled design, as in a border

sgraffito–design made by scratching thru a glaze (usually on pottery) to reveal a different color; effect similar to grisaile

silica–quartz; pure sand is granulated silica

sunstone–a brilliant type of aventurine; see goldstone

tea gold–copper shavings in translucent enamel, as done by the Japanese—"chakin"

translucent–imperfectly transparent

vitreous–like glass, or derived from glass

CHINESE PRONUNCIATION

Much of the literature pertaining to the subject of enamel wares contains terms taken from the native language of China and Japan, but does not provide the English equivalents. A glossary of the most common words used should result in a better understanding and retention of the matter discussed. The accompanying tables are intended to serve this purpose.

The following list of consonants and vowels provides the English equivalents of the Chinese pronunciation and is generally accepted by the Chinese. Note that there appear to be two ways to pronounce *ao* and *ou;* both are given without comment:

VOWELS

Chinese	English	Chinese	English
a	st*a*r, f*a*ther	ia	*y*arn
ai	*ai*sle	ie	si*e*sta
ao	l*ou*d or *ah-for*	ieh	*ye*a
e	b*e*t	ih	b*i*n
ê	*ea*rn	iu	ad*ieu*
êh	m*ay*	o	f*o*r
ei	fr*ei*ght	ou	*ow*e or *oh-you*
en	d*e*n	u	m*u*te
ên	f*u*n	uai	*wy*e
i	mach*i*ne	uei	*wai*t

CONSONANTS

ch	*g*erm	p	*b*at
ch'	*ch*urch	p'	*p*an
k	*g*o	t	*d*am
k'	*k*ing	t'	*t*an

The apostrophe (') shown with a consonant indicates an aspirate —the sound of *h;* that is, a sound combined with or followed by a sound as of *h*. The symbol does not mean that a letter has been omitted; it means that, for example, the word *t'a* would be pronounced more like *t-ha*, not like *tha*. The common consonant, hs, should be pronounced as in hu*sh*.

CHINESE-ENGLISH LIST
OF SYMBOLS

A Fu Jung–Poppy: Twelfth Month
Cathay–China—so called in the Middle Ages
Ch'a Ching–Classical Book on Tea
Chai–Pavilion: a hall mark
Ch'a Hu–Teapot
Chang–Endless Knot, Entrails: Longevity
Ch'ang fu–Ordinary dress
Ch'ao fu–Robe of State
Chi–Cock (Animal of the Zodiac): West
Chiang–Former name of Yangtze River, about 500 B.C.
Chi'ao Yeh–Palm Leaf: Self Education
Ch'ien–Coin: Wealth; with red ribbons: a Charm
Chien–Sword: Wisdom; Victory over Evil
Chi Fu–Dragon Robe
Ch'ih lung–Archaic dragons on bronze vessels
Ch'i Lin–Unicorn: Benevolence, Rectitude
Ch'in–Lute: Marital Bliss, Suppression of Lust
Ching–Mirror
Chin huang–Gold-yellow (figured silk)
Ching-te-chên–Chinese city; factory for imperial porcelain
Ch'ing tzu–Green porcelain; also *Lü t'ze*
Chu–Pearl or Flaming Jewel: Feminine Beauty, etc.
Chu–Bamboo: Longevity (a different symbol)
Chüeh–Tripod, a sacrificial bronze vessel
Chü Hua–Chrysanthemum: Autumn, Tenth Month, Joviality
Chung–Bell: Respect, Obedience, etc.
Chu niao–Scarlet Bird
Chu tai–Pricket Candlestick
Fa hua–Ming pottery and porcelain, in which clay threads are used
    as cloisons

Fa Lun–Wheel: Wheel of the Law (a Buddhist symbol)

Fang Sheng–Lozenge (diamond shape): Victory (head ornament)

Fei tzui–Jadeite, a type of jade used for jewels

Fên-ch'ing–Glaze or pale purple

Feng-huang–Phoenix: Beauty, Goodness, Sun, Peace

Fên Mi–Rice or Millet Grains: Prosperity

Fo Shou–Citron: Wealth, Buddha's hand

Fu–Scrolls (in many forms): Prosperity, Truth

Fu–Bat: Longevity, Happiness

Fugui–Ancient name for the city of Foochow

Fu-lang–Fo-lang, Fa-lan, Falan: Chinese enamels

Fu-lion–Lion or Devil-Dog, also *Tai chih*

Fu Tsun–Wine Pot of bronze

Ho–Crane: Longevity; Bird of the Immortals

Ho Hua–Lotus: Faithfulness (a Buddhist symbol)

Hsi–Character symbol: Married Happiness; Joy Doubled

Hsiang–Elephant: Strength, Sagacity, Prudence

Hsiang lu–Tripod Incense Burner

Hsi Chiao–Horn Cup

Hsi Fan lien–Indian Lotus

Hsing–Stars: Heart of the Emperor, etc.

Hsi So–Cricket: Summer, Courage

Hsiu (Hsiu hua)–Embroidery

Hsi Wang Mu–Queen Mother of the West (Taoist divinity)

Hu–Tiger: Energy, Power (Animal of the Zodiac)

Hu–Jar or Vase

Hua ku–Beaker, tall and vase-like

Hua Lang–Flower Basket: Delusive Pleasures, etc.

Huang or Huang Ho–Yellow River

Hua P'ang–Flower Dish

Hua P'ing–Rare Flower Vase

Hui-sê–Gray in color (porcelain)

Hu Lu–Gourd: Longevity, Necromancy

Hung Fu–Red Bats: Vast Happiness; see *Pien Fu*

Huo–Flames: Fire Spirit, etc.

Hu Tieh–Butterfly: Joy, Conjugal Felicity

Jih–Sun: Yang, Male, Emperor

Ju-i or Jui–Scepter: Prosperity, Magical Powers, etc.

Ju-Yao–Porcelain made in Ju-chon, in Honan province

Ju Yu–Jade

Kanbalu–the ancient name for Peking

Kan-gui–the ancient name for Canton

Kian–Yangtze River

Kin-sai–Hangchow

Ko ku yao lun–Book on Antiquities, A.D. 1387 and 1459

K'o-ssu–Tapestry, fine thread silk and gold

Ko Yao–Crackle-ware pottery, Sung Dynasty

Ku–Vase or beaker of bronze

Kuan liao–Imperial glass, made in Peking

Kuan yao–Imperial pottery or porcelain, made in Peking

Kuei–Incense Burner of bronze, bowl type

Kuei–Tortoise: Longevity, Strength, etc.

Kuei Hua–Mallow Blossom: Ninth Month

Ku Kuei–Scepter

Kun fu–Emperor's coat

Kung Ping–Altar Vase, pear shape

Lan Hua–Orchid Spray

Lang Yao–Apple green or ruby red, on porcelain

Li or Lia Hua–Pear Blossom: Wise Administration, Eighth Month

Liang hei–Bright black, on porcelain

Liang tun–Garden seat

Lien Hua–Lotus Blossom: July (Buddhist symbol)

Lien Pêng–Lotus Pod: Fruitfulness, Offspring

Ling–Plumes or Peacock Feathers: Official Rank

Ling Chih–Fungus: Longevity, Immortality

Liu li–Opaque glass

Liu Teng–Lantern

Lo–Conch Shell: Royalty, Prosperous Voyage

Lu–Deer (in many forms): Riches

Lung–Dragon: Rain, Spring, Emperor, Eternity. Dragons come in different forms and with different names; *Lung* is the general name.

Lung-ch'uan Yao–Celadon ware, porcelain

Ma–Horse: Animal of the Zodiac

Mao–Cat: Protects silk worms, disperses evil spirits

Mei Hua–Prunus or Plum Blossom: Winter

Mei Ping–Vase, high shouldered, of porcelain or cloisonné

Ming–Title of a dynasty; literally, means "luminous"

Ming Huang–Eighth century emperor or Bright Yellow

Mi se–Yellow glaze on porcelain

Mu Lan–Magnolia: Feminine Sweetness, May (Fifth Month)

Mu Tan–Tree Peony: Spring, Riches, Honor, Third Month

Nien-hac–Name given to the reign of an emperor

Niu–Ox: Animal of the Zodiac

Pa chi hsiang–The Eight Buddhist Emblems of Fortune

Pai Ch'an–Gardenia: November, the Eleventh Month

Pai Ting–Pottery white as flour; also *Fen Ting*
Pa Kua–Eight Trigrams of Divinition—in circle
Pang Shih–Rocks: Permanence, Solidity
Pa'n K'uei–Dragon; see *Lung*
Pao–Leopard: Bravery, Martial Ferocity
Pao Ping–Rare Vase: Perpetual Harmony
Pa Pao–The Eight Precious Things
Pi–Writing Brushes: Scholar
Pi–Green Jade Disc, Chou dynasty
Pien Fu–Bat: Happiness, Longevity; see also *Hung Fu*
Ping–Tripod, bronze
P'ing–Vase: Perpetual Harmony, etc.
Ping kuo ch'ing–Apple green, porcelain color; see *lut'ze*
Po Lan–Waves: Abode of Dragons
P'o-li–Glass, colorless
Po-shan–City in Shantung, noted for glassware, etc.
P'u-fu–Coat
San–Umbrella: Respect, Purity
Shan–Fan: Revives Soul of the Dead
Shan–Mountains: Place of Worship
Shang Hu–Coral: Longevity, etc.
Shê–Serpent: Animal of the Zodiac
Shên Mien–Sacred Disc: Symbol of Heavenly Perfection
Shê-p'i lu–Snake-skin green, color on porcelain
Shih–Lion: Valor; see *Fu-lion* and *Tai chih*
Shih–Persimmon: Joy (different Chinese character)
Shih Liu–Pomegranate: Fruit, Offspring
Shou–Chinese script character: Longevity (many forms)
Shou Lao–God of Longevity
Shou Lu–Monster Urn, or Incense Burner in form of monster
Shu–A Pair of Books: Learning
Shu–Bat: Animal of the Zodiac
Shuang Yü–Fish (a pair): Marriage, Fertility, Conjugal Felicity
Shuang Hsi–Double or Wedded Joy; inscription on bridal gifts
Shu Ching–Classic of History; a book of art
Shui P'ing–Vase, bottle shaped
Sung–Pine Tree: Longevity
Ta Fang P'ing–Vase, tall and four-sided
Tai Chih–Monster lion
Ta lu–Emerald green, on porcelain
Tan Tsao–Pomegranate Blossom: June, Sixth Month
Tao–Peach: Springtime, Marriage, Immortality
T'ao–Ancient character for pottery

Tao Hua–Peach Blossom: Charm against Evil
T'ao T'ieh–Ogre Mask or Water Buffalo head: Gluttony, Avarice
Ta Shih Yao–"Arabian Ware"—cloisonné enamels
Tien Lung–Celestial Dragon; see *Lung*
Ting–Bronze Tripod—ancient ritual vessel
Ting Yao–Pottery, crackled (Sung: creamy white)
Tsao–Pondweed, Watergrass: Spirit of the Water
T'sun–Vase
Ts'ung-lu–Onion green, on porcelain
T'u–Hare: Animal of the Zodiac
Tui–Bronze jar
Tung Chüeh–Bronze Wine Cup: Ancestral Worship
T'u Ting–Yellowish-clay tint, in pottery
T'zu–Porcelain, Han dynasty (original name)
Wa–Earthenware, see *t'ao* or *yao*
Wan, Wan Shou–Swastika: Infinity, The Mind, 10,000, etc.
Wang–King
Wei–Branch of the Yellow (Huang) River
Wei Luo–Historical work on opaque glass, 2nd century
Wo Ts'an–Silkworm: Industry
Wu ts'ai–Ming porcelain, decorated in colors
Ya–Duck: Felicity, Conjugal Fidelity
Yang–Goat: Animal of the Zodiac
Yang T'zu–"Foreign Porcelain" (art of painting, etc.)
Yang Yin–Dual Principle; also written *Yin-Yang*
Yao–Pottery; also means kiln
Yao-pien–Glaze, mottled, on porcelain
Yeh Chi–Pheasant: Beauty, Good Fortune
Yen–Inkstone: Attribute of a Scholar
Ying Hua–Cherry Blossom: Feminine Beauty, Fourth Month
Ying-Lung–Winged Dragon; see *Lung*
Yin Yang–Dual Principle, Male and Female
Yu–Covered Winepot or Jar
Yu–Glaze on Chinese procelain
Yu–Jade and gems
Yueh–Moon with Hare: Female, Passiveness, etc.
Yueh-pai–Clair de lune glaze, pale gray-blue
Yu Kuo–Glaze essence, as Petuntze
Yun–Clouds: Beneficial Rain

NOTE: Sometimes the same Chinese word has two different Chinese characters. The gift of a Chinese or Japanese object of art carries with it the wish for the good fortune implied by the symbols shown on it.

JAPANESE-ENGLISH LIST
OF SYMBOLS

※*・*・*・*・*・*・*・*・*※

The Japanese vowels are pronounced approximately as follows: ā as in father; ē as in grey; i as in brief; ō as in bone; u as in cute.

Akasuké–Enamel, transparent red, on copper, without cloisons; carved

Ando Jubei–Ando Cloisonné Company, Nagoya and Tokyo

Bon–Tray, enameled design usually on both sides

Botan–Peony Moutan, Tree Peony (usually flower only, crimson colored)

Chakin–Tea gold; copper shavings in translucent enamel

Chakra–Wheel of the Law, similar to Chinese *Lun*

Chatsubo–Tea jar, with cover

Chawan–Cup, metal or porcelain, both sides enameled

Cho–Butterfly

Doro-Jippo–Opaque enamel work (*Jippo* same as *Shippo*)

Foo–Phoenix or Bird of Paradise

Fudetate–Jar or round vessel; brush holder

Fuji–Wisteria Chinensis, favorite flower in Japanese art; symbol of early summer

Fuku–Script character in circle: Prosperity

Futasuki no hachi–Covered Bowl (also hachi)

Gin Bari–Transparent enamel on copper base covered with silver "paper" or foil

Gin-Jippo–Transparent enamel, silver base and cloisons

Go-down–Storehouse for precious possessions

Hachi–Basin or shallow bowl, enameled inside and out

Hanaike–Flower Vase

Hari–Crystal

Hayashi Kodenji–Noted cloisonné artist, Nagoya, about 1880
Hikoshiro–Early Shippo maker, for Emperor Tokugawa
Hiyotai–Gourd used for Saki (the drink); a symbol
Hina–One of the Six Seasons celebrated in Japan
Ho-ho–Ancient mythical bird, related to the Phoenix; sometimes called the Flowery Bird
Ikeda–Cloisonné maker, Kyoto
Inaba–Inaba Cloisonné Company, Kyoto and Tokyo
Jippo–Shippo, when combined with a descriptive word
Jiu–Script character: Longevity (various forms)
Judsu–Collection of beads; a Japanese rosary
Kaji Tsunekichi–Artist in Toshima (near Nagoya), discovered how to make cloisonné enamels, about 1839
Kakitsubata–Iris, plant or flower
Kandotshuri–Sake Bottle
Kara Kusa–Pondweed, "China Grass." Ornamental vine, popular in cloisonné decoration
Kara Shishi–Chinese lion; see also Japanese *kirin*
Kibisho–Teapot
Kiji–Pheasant
Kiku–Chrysanthemum, special flower for Festival of Happiness (16-petal used in Imperial crest)
Kin-Jippo–Transparent enamel on gold base
Kiri–Crest or symbol: Emperor Tree (Paulownia imperialis), three flowers with three leaves
Kirin–Lion-like imaginary animal (the offspring of a dragon and a cow)
Kiyojoku–Stand or table, enameled
Kodai-moyo–Old Chinese-like design with kara kusa, and heavy cloisons
Koi–Carp (not to be confused with *Tai*)
Kozara–Plate or small dish, enameled on both sides
Kujaku–Peacock (imported but became a native)
Kumeno Teitaro–Artist in cloisonné enamels, Nagoya
Kusudama–Hanging flower basket
Kwashibachi–Covered bowl or cake bowl
Kwashuri–Cake box
Matsu–Pine Tree: Longevity and Happiness
Meiji–Name of the period of the reign of Emperor Mutsuhito, 1868–1912. "Enlightened Peace"
Meno–Agate
Midzusashi–Water Pot

Mitsu Tomove–Circular emblem, similar to Chinese *Yang-Yin*

Moriagé–Cloisonné enamel, enamel slightly raised

Musen-Jippo–Enamel work without cloisons, a general term

Namakawa Yasuyuki–Famous cloisonné artist, Kyoto

Namakawa Susuke–Tokyo artist, died 1911, famous for method of covering large surface, no cloisons, one color

Nagare Gusuri–Rainbow-colored, porcelain-like glaze on enamel work, perfected by Kawade

Nagoya–Japanese City, famous for cloisonné enamels

Ondori–Cock, common Japanese domestic fowl

Oranda Yaki–"Dutch ware," another name for cloisonné

Oshidori–Mandarin Duck; also *Kinmodsui*

Oumai–Plum Tree and the blossoms, symbolic of Spring

Rosokutate–Candlestick, pricket type

Ruri–Glass, or a green gem

Saiyu Shippo–Embossed metal, enameled (Ando Cloisonné Co.)

Sake–Japanese drink, brewed from rice

Sakura–Cherry Tree, cultivated for its flowers

Sara–Dish, in cloisonné enamels

Sentoku–Cast bronze

Shako–Coral

Shibu-ichi–Copper and silver inlay, various proportions

Shippo–Treasures; cloisonné enamels

Shippo Yaki–Another name for Shippo

Shakuyaku–Plant and flower, similar to the Peony

So-chiku-bai–Combination name for Pine, Bamboo and Plum Trees

Shogun–Japanese military governor

Shoso-in–Storehouse for Imperial Treasure, eighth century

Shotai-Jippo–Enamel without base, like stained glass window

Shuro–Brazier

Suki-Jippo–Translucent enamel

Tai–Red-skinned salt-water fish, one of the seven Japanese household deities

Taka–Falcon; appears only in enamels

Taka–Sacred Jewel

Take–Bamboo Tree, symbol of a long and happy life

Tatsu–Dragon, three-toed, similar to Chinese dragon

Tokuri–Bottle with round body, long neck

Tokyo–Japanese city, famous for cloisonné enamels

Tomeiyu Shippo–Transparent cloisonné enamels (Ando Cloisonné Co.)

Toro–Lamp for Buddhist temple.

Toshima–Village near Nagoya, known as *Shippo Mura* or "Village
  of cloisonné wares"
Totai Shippo–Enamels with transparent insets (Ando Cloisonné Co.)
Tsinki–Hammered metal, made into a design
Tsuba–Sword hilt
Tsubakura–Swallow, a popular bird in enamel work
Tsuru–Crane, white or gray: Longevity
Uchidashi–Cloisonné on relief-hammered metal base
Uguisu–Nightingale
Uma–Horse
Usuji–Enamel ground is light and in one color
Washi–Eagle; appears only on cloisonné enamels
Yoshi–Reeds in water, shown with ducks
Yusen-Jippo–Ordinary enamel work, with cloisons
Zo–Elephant
Zogan Shippo–Champlevé enamels (Ando Cloisonné Co.)

MELTING POINTS OF METALS AND OTHER MATERIALS

MELTING OR FUSING POINT

Element	Fahrenheit	Centigrade	Remarks
Aluminum	1220°	660°	
Antimony	1166	630.5	
Brass	1859	1015	varies; copper/zinc
Britannia metal	(see white metal)		tin/copper/antimony
Bronze	1800–1868	982–1020	copper 80–95%; balance, tin
Copper	1981	1083	
Gilding metal	1950	1065	gold with mercury amalgam
Glass	1800–2900	982–1593	depends on composition
Glass enamels	1450–1550	788–845	depends on composition
Gold, 24k	1945	1063	
Iron	2795	1535	
Lead	621	327	
Magnesium	651	343	
Manganese	1244	673	
Mercury	−102	−39	freezing point
Nickel	2646	1452	
Pewter	500	360	average tin to lead: 5 to 1
Platinum	3192	1754	
Porcelain	2300–2600	1260–1427	
Pottery (clay)	1450	788	
Quartz (silica)	3110	1710	
Silver (fine)	1761	960	silver, 99%
Silver (sterling)	1652	898	silver, 92.5%; copper, 7.5%
Solder (silver)	1335	723	silver, 10%; copper/zinc

Element	Fahrenheit	Centigrade	Remarks
Solder (soft)	356–440	188–227	tin and lead, varies
Speculum metal	1800±	982±	copper, 67%; tin, 33%
Tin	450	232	
Water	212	100	boiling point
White metal	1000±	538±	tin, 90%; antimony, 10%
Zinc	787	419	

CONVERSION FACTORS: Fahrenheit degrees equals $9/5$ Centigrade degrees plus 32. Centigrade degrees equals Fahrenheit degrees minus 32 times $5/9$. Example: Water, F° is $9/5$ times 100 plus 32 equals 212°.

Bibliography

As stated in the Preface, many of the following references are either out of print or are not available in the local libraries. It is usually possible for a library to borrow the required book or magazine from another which does have a copy in its files.

A ten-year search in various large libraries (New York, Boston, St. Louis, Cambridge) produced little of additional value on the present subject. A brief description of the contents of those references which were found to provide useful information is therefore given for each one listed:

1. Bates, Kenneth F., *Enameling: Principles and Practice*. World Publishing Co., Cleveland, 1951. A practical book on the description, design, and making of modern enamels. Many good illustrations of work done in Germany, France, Byzantium, and China.
2. Batsford, B. T., editor, *Chinese Art*. B. T. Batsford Ltd. London, "Printed in Czechoslovakia," no date (probably about 1950). Essays on the aesthetic virtues of various kinds of Chinese art as compared to English art. Well illustrated; contains two good sketch maps of China.
3. Bovin, Murray, *Jewelry Making*. Forest Hills, New York, 1959. A modern well-written book giving a practical description of the process of making cloisonné enamels; includes data on proportions of ingredients, temperatures, and other details.
4. Bowes, James L., *Japanese Enamels*. "Printed for Private Circulation," Liverpool, 1884. This is probably the best book on the sub-

ject of Japanese cloisonné work, but it is rare. Good illustrations show design, symbolism, and identification.

5. Bowes, James L., *Notes on Shippo-a sequel to Japanese enamels.* Paul, London, 1895. An addition to Bowes' "1884 Essay"; not as complete but much more available.

6. Bushell, Stephen W., M.D., *Chinese Art*, two volumes. Victoria and Albert Museum Handbooks, London, six editions—1904 to 1921. The most instructive, reliable, readable treatise covering the many forms of Chinese art, including enamels. Good illustrations.

7. Encyclopedia Britannica, "China," various editions. An extensive descriptive summary of the geography, history, people, and arts of China. Provides a good background to the following reference.

8. "Enamels." A well-written compilation of articles, from several sources, on the history and description of enamels in various countries. The extensive excerpt from Dr. Bushell's treatise on Chinese enamels, Vol II) is especially valuable. See no. 6, above.

9. Fisher, Alexander, "Art of True Enameling on Metals," *International Studio Magazine*, Vols. 13, 14, 16 (March 1901 to June 1902). History and description of various kinds of enamels— mainly of work done in England.

10. Garner, Sir Harry, *Chinese & Japanese Cloisonné Enamels.* Charles E. Tuttle Company, Rutland, Vermont, 1962. An erudite treatise, with good illustrations, mostly on the subject of Chinese enameled ware in English museums. Includes a short discussion of Japanese enamels and of related work by other authors.

11. Getz, John, compiler, *Catalogue of the Avery Collection of Ancient Chinese Cloisonnes.* Museum of the Brooklyn Institute of Arts and Sciences, Brooklyn, New York, 1912. This book covers the description of 145 outstanding examples of Chinese enamels; there are many excellent black-and-white illustrations. The catalogue contains a long excerpt taken from Vol. II of *Chinese Art* by Dr. S. W. Bushell [6] and is more readily available than the original.

12. Grousset, Rene, *Chinese Art and Culture*, A. Deutch, London, 1959. An exceptionally well-written and annotated book, with an extensive bibliography. Describes the various kinds of art in China, including history and symbolism. Good illustrations, but not keyed to the text.

13. Harada, Jiro, "Japanese Art and Artists of Today," *International Studio Magazine*, Vols. 41, 42, 43, 44 (1910, 1911). Sec. VI in Vol. 44 (October 1911) discusses cloisonné enamels in unusually precise detail, with excellent illustrations. The best and most reliable of all references on Japanese work.

14. Hawley, W. H., *Chinese Art Symbols, #12,* H. W. Hawley, Hollywood, Calif., 1945. A pictorial chart of 160 items, each with the Chinese and English name and the meaning of each symbol. One of a series of charts on Oriental culture.

15. *Chinese Dragons,#13,* H. W. Hawley, Hollywood, Calif., 1946. A pictorial chart showing 41 Chinese dragons, each with the Chinese and English name and the corresponding symbol.

16. Hobson, H. L., "Chinese Enamels." *Burlington Magazine,* Vol. 21 (June to August, 1912), three-part article. Also, "A Note on Canton Enamel," Vol. 22 (1913). A well-written account of enameling, both cloisonné and porcelain, with good illustrations.

17. MacKensie, Finlay, *Chinese Art,* Marboro Books, New York, by arrangement with Books for Pleasure, Ltd., London, 1961. A brief account of China and its art. Excellent colored photographs of pottery and painting (41 of the 48 pieces are in English museums).

18. Palmer, R. R., editor. *Atlas of World History,* Rand McNally & Company, New York, 1957. A series of instructive maps, with a descriptive text, to show major changes in world history from about 500 B.C. Also published without the accompanying text, 1961.

19. Polo, Marco. *The Travels of Marco Polo.* There are various editions; a good one is by Manuel Komroff, Garden City Publishing Co., Inc.-Copyright 1930 by Horace Liveright, Inc. A fantastic but true account of the extensive travels and experiences of Marco Polo, late in the 13th century, in China and southeastern Asia. Provides an interesting background to more definitive studies.

20. Prodan, Mario. *Chinese Art.* Pantheon, New York, 1958. A general history and description of the various kinds of Chinese art, back to ancient times. He makes the interesting statement that China has produced no real art in the past 400 years, that all real art objects date from prior to about 1550.

21. Royal Ontario Museum of Archaeology. *Chinese Court Costumes.* Toronto, 1946. Although confined to textiles, such as silken court robes, it is a well-written treatise on design, color, and symbolism as evolved by the Chinese from ancient times. It contains colored illustrations, symbols, and various tables.

22. Silcock, Arnold. *Introduction to Chinese Art and History.* Oxford University Press, New York, 1948. One of the best books on the general history of Chinese arts, methods of working, materials and symbolism. Instructive maps and a table of pronunciation of Chinese words.

23. Smith, Ray Winfield. "History revealed in Ancient Glass," *Na-*

tional Geographic Magazine, Sept. 1946. A description of modern
methods used to determine the origin and age of ancient glass.

24. "The Springfield [Mass.] Art Museum and The George Walter
    Vincent Smith Collection." *Western New England Magazine*,
    March, 1913. Describes and illustrates a large and valuable collec-
    tion of Chinese and Japanese art. Superb examples of cloisonné
    enamels are on permanent display in the museum-an exception to
    the present fashion of most of the country's large museums.

25. Untracht, Oppi. *Enameling on Metal*. Chilton Company, Philadel-
    phia, 1959. Undoubtedly the best book on modern enameling pro-
    cesses on all kinds of metals. Detailed instructions, many photo-
    graphs, tables of ingredients, melting points, etc. Provides valuable
    information to the collector of enameled ware.

26. Upson, Arthur. "The Art of Shippo Yaki." *International Studio
    Magazine*, Vol. 30 (January, 1907). Well written and with good il-
    lustrations.

27. Willette, William. *History of China*. Penguin Books, two volumes,
    Baltimore, 1958. Includes a discussion and many drawings of every
    category of Chinese art except enameled wares.

Index

Subject index. See also the Appendices.

age of enamel making, 10, 12, 20, 21, 23-26, 30
age of glass making, 15, 19, 20, 21, 50
Akasuké, 68
Ando Cloisonne Co., 12, 67
antimony, 14, 17
antique, definition of, 11
Arabian ware, 24, 37
astronomical observatory, 3
aventurine, 80

Bakin, 74
bats, 45, 84
birds, 62, 75, 78
Bowes, James L., 6, 7, 9, 11, 70
brass, 30, 32, 33
Brinkley, Frank, 10, 69
bronze, 4, 22, 32-34, 37, 59, 60, 83
Buddhism, 44, 77, 85
Bushell, Stephen W., 8, 18, 21, 22, 24, 58, 70
butterfly, 45, 77
Byzantium, 20, 21, 24, 37

calendar, Chinese, 1
Canton enamels, 37
Cathay, 3, 22
celadon, 56
Celts, 20
ceramic ware, 35, 54
Chakin, 80
champlevé, 15, 20, 25, 28, 29, 33, 83

Cheney, Sheldon, 9
Chen Lin-son, 9
cherry blossom, 45, 46, 103
Ch'ien Lung, 26
Ch'in, 1
china grass, 46, 73
Ch'ing, 4
Ching T'ai, 25
Ching-te-chen, 56, 58
chinoiserie, 58
Chou, 1, 38
chronology, Chinese arts, 22
chrysanthemum, 7, 75, 85
clay and china, 55
cloisonné, 15, 20, 26, 28, 30-33, 63
cloisonné-on-porcelain, 70, 71
cloisons, 12, 30, 31, 33, 34, 47, 48
clouds, 46, 85
color of enamels, 16, 17, 34, 49-51, 56, 57, 79, 80
Constantinople, 20
copper, 32, 33, 66, 80, 83
cosmic order, 40
cost, Japanese enamels, 12
counter-enamel, 66
crane, 78
craze, 66

dates, determination of, 25, 26
design, 37, 38, 53, 72
devil dog, 84
devil mask, 44
"devils' country," 23, 24
diaper patterns, 73, 84

Distinction: Chinese vs Japanese, 82-85
Doro-jippo, 64
dragon, 39-43, 47, 74

earthenware, 54, 55
Egyptians, 19, 69
elephant, 84
Emperor Tree, 76
enamel on porcelain, 69-71
enamels, Chinese, 10, 11, 15, 21-23, 25, 28-35
enamels, Japanese, 63-78, 80, 81
Endless Knot, 84

Falan, 23, 28
famille rose, 57
famille verte, 57
filigree, 35
flames, 47
flowers, 45, 77
flux, 16, 17
foil, silver, 64, 67, 81, 84
Fo-lang, 24
frit, 16, 17
Fu-lin, 23, 28, 63
fu-lion, 44

Garner, Sir Harry, 7, 11, 50
Gin-bari, 64, 67
Gin-jippo, 64
glass, 13, 14, 19-21, 26, 67
glaze, 20, 57, 69
glue, orchid, 65
goldstone, 81
Grand Canal, 3
Great Wall of China, 3
Greek art and sculpture, 20
green enamel, 79, 85
gres, 55

Han dynasty, 1, 2, 7, 21, 39, 43, 55
Harada, Jiro, 7, 9, 10, 11, 63, 64, 80
Hart, Mrs., 65
Ho-ho Bird, 75
Hsia, 37
human figures, 53
Huns, 2

illustrations, cloisonné enamels, 32
Imperial yellow, 50
Inaba Cloisonne Co., 12
Istanbul, 20
ivory, 10, 59, 60

Jade, Jadeite, 4, 22, 58, 59
Japan, 5, 6
Japanese enamels, 6, 7

Kaji Tsunekichi, 12, 63, 67
K'ang Hsi, 26, 57
kaolin, 56
Karakorum, 2
kara kusa, 73, 77
kazari-jippo, 69
Khan, Genghis or Jenghis, Kublai, 2, 3
kiku crest, 75, 85
Kin-jippo, 64
kiri crest, 76, 85
kirin, 73, 78
Kodai moyo, 68
Ko ku yao lun, 23, 49
Korea, 6, 68, 72
Kuei kuo yao, 23, 24
Kunming, 24
Kyoto, 7, 48, 96
Kyoto-jippo, 64, 68

Lac, 61
lacquer, 22, 27, 61
lapis lazuli, 49, 50
lion, 44, 73, 84
lotus, 77, 85

magnesium, 14, 15
magnolia, 7
making enamels, Chinese, 27-35
making enamels, Japanese, 63-71
Manchus, Manchuria, 1, 4
manganese, 14, 15
mark (date), 25
melting points, 14, 16, 17, 33, 55, 65
metal oxides, 13, 17, 57
Ming dynasty, 4, 8, 12, 23, 25, 34, 50, 53, 57
Mongols, Mongolia, 2, 21-23
months, Chinese, 45
Moriagé, 68
Musen-jippo, 64, 67

Nagare-gusuri, 64
Nagashi-jippo, 69
Nagoya, 7, 48
Namakawa, Kyoto, 70
Namakawa, Yasuyuki, 71
Nanking, 3
Nara, 7
National Geographic Magazine, 15, 19
Nature worship, 38
Nephrite, 58

obsidian, 13
ogre, 38, 44, 84
opaque glass and enamel, 14, 17, 83
Orandi-yaki, 63
orchid glue, 65

painted enamels, 28, 50, 83
painting, Chinese, 22, 49
Paris Exhibition, 5
Paris Exposition, 11
paste, enamel, 31, 34
Paulownia Tree, 76
peach blossom, 45, 85
Peiping (alternate name for Peking—1928 to 1940)
Peking (Kanbalu, Khanbaligh, Tatu, Peiping), 1, 3, 24, 26
peony, 7, 77, 85
Perry, Commodore, 5
petuntse, 56
Phoenix, 39, 40, 43, 75, 84
pigtail, 4
pinholes in enamel, 34, 35, 88
Plique-à-jour, 68
plum, 46, 77
polishing enamel, 29, 31, 87
Polo, Marco, 2, 3, 4, 22, 24, 26
pondweed, 46, 85
porcelain, 22, 35, 36
pottery, 54
Priest, Alan, 54
prunus, 45, 46, 77

Quadrants, Four, 39
quartz, 14, 80

Rand McNally, 24

sang de beouf, 50
script, Chinese, 41, 48
scrolls, 47, 84, 85
Seasons, Four, 39
Shang, 1
Shibataro Kawade, 67
Shippo, 10, 12, 63, 67, 69
Shippo-yaki, 10, 63
Shotai-jippo, 64, 67
silica, 13, 14
silk, 22, 26
silver, 16, 30, 32, 81
Six Dynasties, 2
Smith, Ray Winfield, 15, 19
Smith Collection, Springfield, Mass., 6, 26
solder, 33, 34, 65, 66

sparkle, 80, 81, 84
spirals, 47
stoneware, 55
Suki-jippo, 64
Sung dynasty, 56, 57
Sunstone, 80
Swastika, 85
sword guards, 6, 79, 80
symbolism, 37-39, 47, 53, 72

T'ang dynasty, 2, 56
Tartar or Tatar, 2, 3
Tatu, *see* Peking
temperatures, 14, 17, 55
Temuchin, 2
tiger, 39, 40
tin, 17, 29, 32
Tokugawa, 6
Tokyo, 7, 12, 67
Toledo Art Museum, 21
trade with Japan, 5
Trigrams, Eight, 40, 41
Tsunekichi, Kaji, 12, 63, 67
turquoise blue, 50
turtle, tortoise, 39, 40
tz'u, 55

Uchidashi, 68
Universe, 40, 41
Untracht, Oppi, 16
Usuji, 68

Venice, 20
vitreous, 13, 34

water clocks, 3
waves, 46, 85

Yang and Yin, 38-41
Yangtze River, 1, 39
Yellow River, 1, 39
Yüan dynasty, 3, 4, 23
Yung Cheng, 26, 58
Yunnan province, 1, 24
Yusen-jippo, 64

zinc, 32
zoology, 38